First in their Hearts

A Biography of George Washington

AMERICAN ★ CAVALCADE

First in
their Hearts

A Biography of George Washington

★

THOMAS FLEMING

MARSHALL CAVENDISH
CORPORATION

GREY CASTLE PRESS

Published by Grey Castle Press, Lakeville, Connecticut.

Marshall Cavendish Edition, North Bellmore, New York.

Published in large print and condensed by arrangement with Walker and Company.

Printed in the USA.

Library of Congress Cataloging-in-Publication Data

Fleming, Thomas J.
    First in their hearts : a biography of George Washington / by Thomas Fleming.
        p.   cm.— (American cavalcade)
    Originally published : New York : Walker, 1967.
    Includes bibliographical references and index.
    Summary: A biography of the surveyor, militia major, and aide to the British General Braddock who became leader of the American forces during the Revoltion and first president of the new nation.
    ISBN 1-55905-099-3 (lg. print)
    1. Washington, George, 1732–1799—Juvenile literature.   2. Presidents—United States—Biography—Juvenile literature.   3. Large type books.   [1. Washington, George, 1732–1799.   2. Presidents.   3. Large type books.]   I. Title.   II. Title:—1st in their hearts.   III. Series.
[E312.66 F55 1991]
973.4'1'092—dc20
[B]
[92]   90-48979
                                                                                                CIP
                                                                                                AC

ISBN 1-55905-099-3
      1-55905-100-0 (set)

Photo Credits:

Cover: Library of Congress
The Mount Vernon Ladies' Association—pgs. 45, 101, 135 (top), 135 (bottom)
North Wind Picture Archives—pgs. 21, 34, 131, 143
The Bettmann Archive—pgs. 14, 63, 83
Brown Brothers—pg. 171

Contents

1

A Raw Laddie

ALL THROUGH THE BITTER December day the two men labored beside the turbulent ice-choked Allegheny River, hacking down trees with their single small hatchet and lashing the logs into a raft. One of them was a smallish, average-looking man, a veteran frontiersman named Christopher Gist. The other was a young giant named George Washington.

He stood six feet two and one-half inches in an age when disease and poor diets kept most men a half-foot shorter. His arms and legs were exceptionally long and his hands were twice the size of those of an ordinary man. Amazing strength flowed into them from his massive shoulders.

Washington needed every ounce of this physical prowess on the day he challenged the icy Allegheny. The place where he and Gist built their raft is now within the city limits of Pittsburgh. In 1753, it contained mile after unmapped mile of dense forest, thick with giant black walnut, cherry, oak, and locust trees and tangled creepers. Both men were exhausted by days of tramping through cold so fierce the small streams froze solid, and it was impossible to find drinking water. Finally, as the sun sank behind the western hills, the raft was ready, and they poled away from the bank to begin a wild voyage.

They were in trouble from the first moment. Even Washington's strength was helpless against the river's black, violent current. In desperation, Washington shoved his pole straight down to the bottom, hoping to hold the raft against the current until they saw an opening in the thundering, crunching stream of ice.

He had badly underestimated the river's power. The moment his pole touched bottom, the raft spun in a wild circle, and he was pitched headfirst into the dark, freezing water. The raft swirled past. At the last possible moment, one of Washington's long arms shot out, and his big hand caught a projecting log. Swearing vigorously, he dragged himself back aboard the raft.

Desperate now, his clothes soaked in the below-freezing cold, he saw they could neither advance nor retreat. He ordered Gist to pole for a small barren island in the center of the river. They stumbled ashore and spent a long frigid night there, without even wood to make a fire. In the first gray light of dawn, he peered at the river. With a whoop of joy he shouted good news to his unhappy comrade. The watery foe was frozen solid. They could walk across!

George Washington was twenty-one years old when he survived this bout with the Allegheny River. He was on the last leg of a thousand-mile journey through a winter wilderness with a message that began a world war. The daring Siegneurs of Imperial France had armed and inflamed the Indians and had built a fort in English territory, south of Lake Erie, preparing the way to claim the vast Ohio Valley for their King. Robert Dinwiddie, the Royal Governor of Virginia, decided to send them an ultimatum demanding retreat and threatening war. In all Virginia, he could find only one volunteer: a ''raw laddie,'' as the old Scot called him, named George Washington.

The green volunteer proved himself the equal of veteran frontiersmen like the forty-four-year-old Gist. Swiftly Washington organized and led a seven-man expedition, which covered 500 miles of trackless forest in the worst of winter, and delivered the message to the French commander. Along the way, Washington also negotiated with Indian chiefs and did a little espionage. Meeting a detachment of French soldiers in the forest, he had dinner with them. "They told me it was their absolute design to take possession of the Ohio and by God they would do it," he wrote in his journal.

Washington raced back to Virginia with the news. A few months later, at the age of twenty-two, he was out on the frontier again, leading a regiment, with the rank of lieutenant colonel. When his Indian scouts spotted a French patrol, the impetuous young commander immediately decided to attack. Marching all night, he stealthily surrounded the sleeping enemy. Then with a fearlessness that was to be his trademark as a soldier, Washington strode into the clearing and called for their surrender.

The French reply was a volley in Washington's direction. One man was killed and two were wounded only a few feet away from him. "I heard the bullets whistle," he wrote to his brother Jack the next day, "and believe me there is something charming in the sound."

The Virginians returned the French fire with a hail of bullets from all sides. In fifteen minutes the fight was over. Ten Frenchmen lay dead and twenty-one survivors surrendered. Young Washington was elated. "If the whole detachment of the French," he wrote Governor Dinwiddie, "behave with no more resolution than this chosen party did, I flatter myself we shall have no great trouble in driving them to Montreal.''

The fledgling lieutenant colonel soon regretted his over-confidence. A few weeks later, French reinforcements attacked him and his untrained soldiers in Fort Necessity, a flimsy stockade they had constructed at a place called Great Meadow on the western side of the Allegheny plateau. Hoping to fight a drill-master's war, Washington marched his men out and tried to engage the French in the open field. The French, well trained in forest fighting, scattered behind rocks and tree stumps and poured a withering fire into Washington's compact force.

In a midnight parley, the French offered to let the survivors (almost one-third of Washington's 284 effectives were dead or wounded) march out with their arms, unmolested if they agreed to retire to Virginia. There was really no alternative but to swallow, for the first time, the bitter taste of defeat and surrender. The next day, Washington's battered men straggled toward Virginia. The date, which meant nothing to the unhappy lieutenant colonel for the moment, was July 4th.

For the next seven years France and England grappled for supremacy in Europe, the West Indies, Asia, and America, in a world war begun by Washington's chastening baptism of fire. It is almost uncanny—and forgotten by most Americans—that this oversized young Virginian, born three thousand miles from London and Paris, managed to thrust himself, at twenty-one, onto the center of the world stage. Where did he come from? No one can hope to understand George Washington's amazing career without exploring his boyhood and teenage years.

Surveying a Realm

GEORGE WAS THE THIRD SON of Augustine Washington, a hard-working, fairly wealthy proprietor of some 4,000 Virginia acres and part owner of a busy but unprofitable iron works. Augustine was well educated, having spent most of his youth in England. George, the first-born of Augustine's second marriage, to Mary Ball, would certainly have received the same gentleman's education. But when George was eleven, his father, a big, muscular man who could heft a mass of iron two other men together could not move, suddenly sickened and died.

On that day George Washington became a poor relation. In accordance with English law, the oldest son, Lawrence Washington, inherited the bulk of his father's estate. George was marooned on Ferry Farm, across the river from Fredericks-

Ferry Farm, where George Washington lived from the age of three, overlooked the Rappahannock River in Virginia.

burg, with his mother, a younger sister, and three younger brothers. His mother, Mary Ball, was a large, formidable woman, headstrong and short tempered. Many years later, one of Washington's cousins and boyhood playmates recalled that he was "ten times more afraid" of Mary Ball than he ever was of his own parents. George and this domineering woman were soon at odds.

One day George decided to break for the saddle a particularly difficult young colt. His mother, who was an excellent horsewoman, was undoubtedly on hand to watch the performance. The Ferry Farm colt was tough and determined;

George was more so. For hours the young horse bolted and bucked around the pasture. Nothing could throw the resourceful young rider. Suddenly, gasping a bloody froth, the colt toppled into the dust. The gallant horse's heart had burst.

Perhaps it was in this moment, as she saw the gangling rawboned youth standing over the fallen horse, that Mary Ball realized that she could never dominate George—as she could his brothers and sister. Within a few months after his father's death, George began spending much of his time visiting at the homes of his half brothers, Augustine and Lawrence. "Austin" as Augustine was called, was a likable fellow, fond of good wine, owner of thirty-six fast race horses. It was to twenty-six-year-old Lawrence that George gravitated with a hero worship only a fatherless boy can feel. Lawrence was, first of all, a soldier, having served under Admiral Edward Vernon in the 1741 British expedition against the Spanish treasure city of Cartagena. He renamed the estate left him by his father "Mount Vernon" in honor of his old commander.

Both brothers undoubtedly tried to give George some of the benefits of their English educations. During the winter, however, his mother insisted on his attending a school run by a local minister in Fredericksburg. Already there was a

streak of fierce ambition in the lonely misun-
derstood young man. George soon devoured all
this local school had to offer and was faced with
the prospect of a career managing Ferry Farm—
under his mother's quarrelsome tongue. George
took his troubles to Lawrence, who promptly
hatched a scheme to liberate George from his
mother.

George's great grandfather had been, for a
time, a ship's mate. Why not let George revive
this seafaring tradition, and perhaps when he got
to England, even seek a commission in the Royal
Navy? Urged by Lawrence and several of his most
influential friends, Mary Ball Washington wa-
vered, offering, as one friend wrote to Lawrence,
"trifling objections such as fond and unthinking
mothers naturally suggest." Finally, she called it
"a very bad scheme" and issued a flat no.

By now George was fourteen, and while his
grammar was poor and spelling atrocious, his
flair for mathematics was pronounced. Lawrence
now decided that surveying was a natural avenue
for George's talents—and an equally good excuse
to get away from Ferry Farm. Surveying instru-
ments were no problem. George's father had left
a complete set in his storehouse. In the Virginia of
that era the surveyor was no mere technician. He
was the master mariner of the great surge west-

ward, the key to vast tracts of new land being opened in the region west of the Blue Ridge Mountains.

George was soon hard at work, learning his new profession. By the middle of his fifteenth year he was earning money for his surveys. He was also spending more and more time with Lawrence at Mount Vernon. Lawrence had married, and his bride was the daughter of William Fairfax, master of Belvoir, a handsome house just down the river from Mount Vernon. In the Virginia of George Washington's youth, the name Fairfax meant what Rockefeller means today. Lord Thomas Fairfax was "the Proprietor"—owner by royal decree—of some five million acres of Virginia's fields and forests. William Fairfax was the baron's cousin and agent, responsible for protecting his interests.

In the summer of 1747, Lord Fairfax himself came from England and established himself at Belvoir. As a result, some of the best society in Virginia swirled through this Potomac mansion. George, awkward sixteen though he was, participated in it eagerly. All the Fairfaxes, even dour, difficult Lord Thomas, seem to have treated Lawrence's over-sized younger brother with extraordinary kindness.

Not so kind were the young belles who danced

and flirted with George and the other young men of this highly sociable plantation society. George pursued in vain a number of these elusive beauties and soon found he was suffering from serious disadvantages. To the coldly appraising eye of an affluent Virginia girl his modest inheritance and his lack of English education left him far behind dozens of otherwise equally eligible men. George took his defeats hard, translating some of them into atrocious poetry.

> *Oh ye Gods, why should my poor resistless heart*
>   *Stand to oppose thy might and power*
> *At last surrender to cupid's feathered dart*
>   *And now lays bleeding every hour*
> *For her that's pitiless of my grief and woes*
>   *And will not on me pity take*
> *I'll sleep amongst my most inveterate foes*
>   *And with gladness never wish to wake.*

In a letter to his cousin Robin Washington, George bemoans another setback at the hands of "a lowland beauty." In another letter to "Dear friend John," he tells how he is currently living at Belvoir, where "an agreeable young lady" also lives and constantly "brings the other into my rememberance whereas perhaps were she not often (unavoidably) presenting herself to my view, I might in some measure eleviate my sorrows by burying the other in the grave of oblivion."

But in the midst of romance, adventure beck-
oned. Lord Fairfax was planning an expedition to
map his vast western lands, and young George
was invited to go along as assistant surveyor. He
accepted with alacrity. With him went George
William Fairfax, son of the master of Belvoir,
seven years older than Washington, a personable
young man recently back from schooling in England and already a member of the Virginia
House of Burgesses. Along with making an important friend, George got his first taste of the
frontier. He was so fascinated he began a daily
journal—a habit he was to continue for a lifetime.

Though he had grown up on a farm, young
George admitted he was "not so good a woods-
man" as the others. On his first night on the trail,
he elected to sleep in a nearby tavern, rather than
around the campfire. When he found his bed was
"nothing but a little straw matted together without sheets or anything else but only one thread
bear blanket with double its weight of vermin
such as lice fleas etc" he swiftly put on his clothes
again and "lay as my companions."

A few days later the travelers met an Indian
war party, homeward bound with two scalps, and
later encountered a group of German immigrants
who impressed George as "ignorante . . . they
would never speak English but when spoken to

they speak all Dutch.'' From dawn to dusk Washington surveyed farms of 400 acres for settlers yet to come. He liked the work and he liked the pay even more. He averaged 7 dollars a day. In December of that same year he took a short course at William and Mary College in Williamsburg, passed an examination, and got his first official license as a surveyor. With help from Lawrence and the Fairfaxes, George became the official surveyor of Culpeper County in the summer of his seventeenth year, receiving an annual salary of 100 pounds; and he had spare time to earn more money elsewhere.

For the next three years, young Washington continued to work as a surveyor, sometimes along the frontier for Lord Fairfax, sometimes for other customers, elsewhere. He laid out the lots and streets of a new town, eventually named Alexandria. He was good at his job. Many of his surveys are still on file in Virginia. There is a precision, almost a delicacy, to his lines and arrows that approaches beauty. To keep track of his money, he began an account book, meticulously noting all his expenses and earnings. Sometimes he took payment for his work in land and invested his hard-earned cash in more land.

But there were other, more important, influences in young Washington's life during these

By the age of 16, George was earning money as a surveyor. At 17 he became the official surveyor of Culpeper County.

crucially formative years. He spent almost all his non-working hours at Belvoir and Mount Vernon. In these houses on the remote banks of the Potomac that young colonial George Washington,

acquired an education no school could have supplied. It was superior because it came by example
and reached both the emotions and the mind.

The Fairfaxes, in the great tradition of the English aristocracy, had defended liberty for genera-
tions. The first Lord Fairfax had been a rebel
against Charles I in the English Civil War. Spir-
itually, the Fairfaxes found their inspiration in the
great figures of the ancient Roman Republic.

Lawrence Washington wholeheartedly shared
in this dedication. In one of the few letters that
has survived to give us a glimpse of this young
man, a friend writes to him during the expedition
to Cartagena, urging him to come home and give
up his pursuit of ''the title of honor'' on the
battlefield. The phrase goes to the heart of this
tradition. These men saw life in terms of duty and
honor, both personal and public. No duty was
higher, no honor more glorious, than service to
one's country. A man could not hope to perform
this service well without achieving self-mastery.

Impossibly noble? It may sound that way to
our cynical era. But this philosophy gave hot-
tempered, stubborn young George Washington
goals he would pursue all his life. It opened his
eyes to horizons beyond the sociable whirl of
horse races, fox hunts, dances, and girls that absorbed most young Virginians his age. Other as-

pects of life with the Fairfaxes and his brother Lawrence helped. There was, in the company of these men, a sense of being at the center of things. In the long evening hours, George listened while they discussed plans for an Ohio Company that would settle and develop this vast river valley, claimed by both England and France.

At the end of these four formative years came tragedy. Lawrence, that debonair soldier and thoughtful substitute father, was stricken with tuberculosis and slowly wasted away before the eyes of his grief-stricken family. He was as generous toward his half brother in death as he had been in life. With modest provisos for the support of his wife, who soon remarried, Lawrence left George the Mount Vernon estate.

There is no record of Washington ever telling anyone how deeply he felt Lawrence's loss. As with many other things in his life, his actions spoke louder. As long as George was master of Mount Vernon, Lawrence's portrait remained on his desk in the library. Nor did he ever remove the painting of Admiral Vernon at Cartagena.

3

"Experience, Alas"

LIKE JOHN F. KENNEDY after the death of a much admired and loved older brother, Washington seems to have stepped forward to take Lawrence's place as the family's leader. Though George was only twenty, the Fairfaxes persuaded Virginia's governor to appoint him to Lawrence's post as one of the colony's four militia majors. A few months later George volunteered for the harrowing winter journey to the French fort on Lake Erie. It was obviously something Lawrence would have wanted him to do.

When someone complained that Washington was too young to be a major, the Fairfaxes reportedly replied, "All Washingtons are born old." There would seem to be more than a little truth to the statement. For a man who had just turned twenty-one, Washington displayed an amazing maturity on this expedition. Isolated in the

French fort, he fought a nerve-wracking contest for the loyalty of three powerful Indian chiefs. Normally allies of the English, the chiefs had agreed to accompany him as a show of defiance. Once in the fort, their heads were quickly addled by French brandy, and their allegiance tempted by promises of extravagant presents.

Washington met the challenge head on. He marched into the quarters of the French commander, a courtly nobleman twice his age, and bluntly told him that his interference with the Indians was delaying their departure and was a breach of diplomatic etiquette. Caught off guard, the Frenchman hastily agreed to give the Indians some presents and let them go. The next day, as Washington and his party were boarding their canoes, the French played a last sneaky card. They suddenly produced jugs of brandy and asked the ''Great Chiefs'' if they would like a few drops before they departed.

Washington stepped between the Indians and the brandy and strenuously reminded them of their promise to depart without delay, and they yielded without a word of argument. One of the chiefs, Half King, was so impressed with the young Virginian, he adopted Washington into his Seneca tribe. He also gave him a name, which had previously been won by Washington's great

grandfather during Indian skirmishes in the pre-
ceding century: *Conotocarious,* "Devourer of Vil-
lages."

A few weeks later, Washington faced a far different test. Leaving the rest of the expedition to
stay with the slow-moving pack horses, he took
his second in command, Christopher Gist, and
struck out through the forest on a short cut.
Along the way they picked up an Indian guide.
As they crossed a clearing, the Indian suddenly
whirled and fired at them from point-blank range.

"Are you shot?" Washington cried to Gist.

"No," said Gist.

The bullet had whistled between them.

The Indian ducked behind a tree to reload.
Washington's long legs carried him to the treacherous guide much faster than the Indian could
ram home powder and ball. Washington wrestled
the musket away from him. Gist raised his gun in
the cruel kill or be killed code of the frontier. The
Indian stared at him, waiting for death. Washington struck up Gist's barrel. He could not shoot
a defenseless man. He let the Indian go even
though it forced him and the protesting Gist to
tramp all night in the opposite direction lest their
would-be assassin return with a war party.

If these were marks of maturity, there was
much else in Washington's character during these

years that was painfully raw. He was, for instance, hypersensitive to criticism. He returned from his defeat at Fort Necessity in a black mood, lashing out at anyone and everyone who dared to censure his tactics.

A warrior tormented by defeat, Washington took refuge at Mount Vernon with his brother Jack. There an even worse disaster overtook him. He fell in love with his best friend's wife. George William Fairfax, his frontier companion of surveying days, had brought home to Belvoir a tall slender elegant girl named Sally Cary. Extremely well educated, a rare thing for Virginia women of that era, she was also witty, impudent, and flirtatious.

It was only natural for Washington and his brother to dine frequently at Belvoir, probably, in fact, to spend most of their time there in preference to womanless Mount Vernon, where there were still so many painful memories of Lawrence. Gradually, without realizing it, George Washington found himself in love with Sally Fairfax.

It was an absolutely hopeless, utterly frustrating emotion. Washington, therefore, did the only thing a man of honor could do. He buried the desire deep in himself and tried to forget it. But it was impossible to forget. There was no way to move Belvoir a few dozen miles down the Potomac and escape Sally's bright talk and mocking eyes. The invitations still flowed out to dinners and dances at which Sally would teasingly ask why Colonel Washington was avoiding her.

For the next four years, Washington struggled to master this inner torment. They were years when most men his age married and began raising families and building up their estates. He returned, instead, to the risks and hardships of a soldier's life.

William Braddock, one of England's best generals, arrived with an army of well-trained redcoats to quench the flames of war on the frontier. He offered Washington a position as an aide-de-camp. Washington immediately accepted, but before he could join the general, another woman in his life arrived to harass him. His mother descended on Mount Vernon with a hundred objections to his risking his life once more.

He finally got away from Mary Ball, urging her, according to one story, to have more faith that God would protect him. She pursued him by letter. On the march, Washington was asked to get her "a Dutchman (perhaps to run her farm) and a tub of butter." Patiently he wrote her, addressing her as "Honored Madam," that since he was in the midst of the wilderness, it was impossible to supply her with either item.

He wrote letters to Sally Fairfax, explaining,

somewhat clumsily, that the really important letters would come from her, and he wrote only to
solicit them. But Washington was, no doubt to his
relief, soon absorbed in another experience as
General Braddock's aide: he was arriving at the
first faint realization that he was not English, but
American. It is hard for us to appreciate this
awakening, now. But in the Virginia of Washington's youth, England was "home."

Now, Washington listened as Braddock and his
officers violently voiced their contempt for American incompetence and bad faith. They had, it was
true, good reason. Only a Pennsylvania politician
named Benjamin Franklin seemed faintly inter-
ested in fulfilling promises and contracts for men
and provisions. Nevertheless, Washington refused to let Braddock blame Americans whole-
sale.

Amazingly, Braddock let him get away with it.
There was something about the young George
Washington that pleased older men. Perhaps it
was his frankness, his stubborn honesty; perhaps
it was his rugged masculinity. Again and again in
his youth, older men reached out to give him a
helping hand. Braddock, famous for the brutality
of his discipline, would listen to Washington's
lectures, and only growl, "What think you of this
from a young hand—from a beardless boy?"

A few weeks later, this beardless boy was one

of the few soldiers who kept his head when Braddock's glistening array of redcoats was attacked by a whooping, howling band of French and Indian irregulars. Though he was only six hours from a sickbed, where he had been prostrate with fever for ten days, Washington was all over the chaotic battlefield, carrying Braddock's orders. Two horses were shot out from under him and four bullets passed through his clothes. When Braddock fell, mortally wounded, and the panic became a rout, Washington was among the handful who stayed to remove the dying general from the battlefield and to organize a rear guard.

Braddock's defeat was a turning point in the life of young George Washington. Never again would the colonial soldier worship English military ability. There is an aura of disbelief in his letters home. To his brother Jack, he wrote: ''We have been beaten, shamefully beaten, by a handful of men who only intended to molest and disturb our march . . . Had I not been witness to the fact . . . I should scarcely have given credit to it even now.'' To his mother he wrote assuring her he was alive and added: ''The dastardly behavior of those they call regulars exposed all others that were inclined to do their duty to almost certain death . . . they ran as sheep pursued by dogs.''

A few days later he was back at Mount Vernon

still weak from his illness and the tremendous exertions on the battlefield and during the retreat. On the very night of his arrival there was a letter from Belvoir, written by Sally Fairfax. ''After thanking Heaven for your safe return, I must accuse you of great unkindness in refusing us the pleasure of seeing you this night. I do assure you nothing but our being satisfied that our company would be disagreeable should prevent us from trying if our legs would not carry us to Mount Vernon this night. But if you will not come to us tomorrow morning very early, we shall be at Mount Vernon.'' Ever circumspect, Sally had two other ladies who were visiting at Belvoir sign the letter with her.

There was no time for Sally now. The world war that had begun on the day Washington first heard the bullets sing now came home to Virginia with a vengeance. The remnants of Braddock's army retreated all the way to Philadelphia, leaving Virginia's 350-mile frontier utterly naked before the poised guns and scalping knives of the French and Indians. The colony looked to twenty-four-year-old George Washington to rescue them from this savage holocaust.

Frantic letters from politicians at Williamsburg reached Washington at Mount Vernon. Would he be willing to serve? His answer was an absolute no—unless the Assembly was ready to vote a realistic amount of money for the campaign and give the commander in the field the right to appoint his own officers. Two defeats had gone a long way toward making a professional soldier out of George Washington. The Burgesses listened and promptly voted him everything he wanted: forty thousand pounds, the authorization to raise a thousand men, and a commission as full colonel and commander-in-chief.

Before he could fight the French, he had to fight one more battle with his mother, who again descended on him with a hundred arguments against his return to the Ohio. This time he was more than a little curt with her. He pointed out that he had not sought the command and it would reflect dishonor on him to refuse it, "and that I am sure must or *ought* to give you greater uneasiness than my going."

On the frontier Washington soon found himself in need of all the maturity he could muster. Chaos was the only way to describe the situation. Near riots ensued every time Washington attempted to recruit soldiers. Settlers refused to supply horses, wagons, or provisions to the officers who were trying to protect them. Those men he did manage to scrape together were almost impossible to discipline.

Meanwhile, Indian war parties poured in.

"Every day we have accounts of such cruelties and barbarities as are shocking to human nature," wrote Washington. "It is not possible to conceive the situation and danger of this miserable country." He had seven hundred men—two for every mile of frontier as densely wooded in many places as the Vietnam jungle. Petitions and pleas for help poured in to him. "I solemnly declare," Washington vowed, "if I know my own mind I could offer myself a willing sacrifice to the butchering enemy provided that would contribute to the people's ease."

From Williamsburg there were only soothing words from his friends. "Our hopes, dear George," wrote speaker of the Assembly, Beverly Robinson, "are all fixed on you for bringing our affairs to a happy issue." From his enemies, who now included Governor Dinwiddie, there were cries for investigation of drunkenness and immorality among the officers and troops.

While civilians poured syrup or spat acid, Washington acted. "We have fought some twenty skirmishes and lost near a hundred men killed or wounded." But when it came to dealing with criticism, he showed himself as thin-skinned as ever. He wrote long, wrathful letters back to Williamsburg, accusing the politicians of multiple failures.

On the frontier the war settled down to dull

At the age of 25, when this portrait was painted, Washington was colonel and commander-in-chief of the Virginia militia during the French and Indian War.

attrition. The British recognized that Canada was the heart of French power in North America and the main armies and men fought the big battles in the north. Washington was left behind, the frustrated commander of a minor theater of war. He watched with dismay, totally unaware that he was learning valuable lessons about what to expect from recalcitrant legislators and politicians who thought they were generals.

He was also learning the grim realities of army discipline. When one of his officers was shamefully deserted by the sergeant and men under his command and was shot and scalped by attacking Indians, Washington court-martialed the sergeant and condemned him to death. He had no power under Virginia law to execute the sentence, but he asked the Assembly to give him the power. They promptly passed a bill that enabled him to send the coward to a firing squad. Not long after, he built a gallows ''forty feet high'' and hanged two deserters on it.

However, there were signs that he was weary of war. From the frontier he wrote long letters to his agent in London, ordering new furnishings for Mount Vernon. He was also thinking about marriage, but not as a man in search of romance.

Not many months later on a trip to Williamsburg, Washington stopped at ''The White House,'' a mansion owned by a young widow of seven months, Martha Dandridge Custis. It is the first evidence we have of their meeting. Martha Custis was one of the wealthiest young women in Virginia, with a six-chimneyed house in Williamsburg at which so distinguished a young man as George Washington had undoubtedly called. They soon knew each other well enough to become engaged.

They were almost the same age; Washington was twenty-seven, Martha nine months older. Washington had a house without a wife to run it; Martha had a vast estate that badly needed a good manager. Some cynical biographers of

Washington have seen the match as a business arrangement. It certainly was not in the tradition of high romance. Washington was still struggling to quench his love for Sally Fairfax. Martha was mourning a dead husband by whom she had had four children. But there is ample proof of a genuine affection. A few weeks after his engagement, Washington was off once more for a last campaign in the wilderness. Practically on horseback, he scribbled Martha a tender farewell note in which he described himself as ''your ever faithful and affectionate friend.''

This word, friend, was to recur again and again throughout Washington's long life with Martha Custis. Apparently it summed up for both of them the dimensions of their relationship. Almost forty years later, when Washington came home from his second term as president, he left a packet of Martha's letters behind him in Philadelphia. The woman who found them wrote teasingly about being shocked to find letters addressed to him in a lady's handwriting. Washington replied that if the letters had been opened, ''they would, I am persuaded, have been found to be more fraught with expressions of friendship than of enamoured love.''

A century before Washington's birth, the great English thinker Francis Bacon wrote, ''A man cannot speak to his son but as a father, to his wife but as a husband . . . whereas a friend may speak as the case requires.'' In Martha Custis, whose good disposition and good sense are evident in her pert, lively face, George Washington found such a friend.

Moreover, Washington was learning, from cruel experience, the truth enunciated by a Roman writer, Seneca, ''. . . friendship always benefits; love sometimes injures.'' Less than four weeks after he vowed his devotion to Martha, he was slogging through the western wilderness once more, and a letter arrived from Sally Fairfax. With that mocking, elusive vein Sally preferred, she teased him over his complaints at the slow progress of the campaign. Was it because he had become a votary of love? Apparently Sally did not realize she was playing along the rim of a human volcano. What came back to her from the wilds was nothing less than an explosion—a long, searching, jumbled cry of anguish from a reticent man who could bury his love no longer:

Tis true I profess myself a votary of love. I acknowledge that a lady is in the case and further I confess that this lady is known to you. Yes, Madame, as well as she is to one who is too sensible to her charms to deny the power whose influence he feels and must ever submit to. I feel the force of her amiable beauties and the recollection of a thousand tender passages that I could wish to obliterate till I am bid to revive them. But experience, alas, sadly reminds me how impossible this is.

You have drawn me, dear madame, or rather I have drawn myself into an honest confession of a simple fact. Misconstrue not my meaning; doubt it not nor expose it. The world has no business to know the object of my love declared in this manner to you when I want to conceal it . . . but adieu to this till happier times, if I shall ever see them.

In this welter of indirection and hinted meanings, necessary lest some stranger read the letter, George Washington is undoubtedly crying out one last time to Sally Fairfax ''I love you. Do you love me?'' As always, Sally was discreet. Her answer was apparently indirect, perhaps cautionary. The letter is lost. We have only Washington's answer.

Do we still misunderstand the true meaning of each other's letters? I think it must appear so tho I would fain hope the contrary as I cannot speak plainer without—but I'll say no more and leave you to guess the rest.

Four months later he married Martha Custis and brought her home to Mount Vernon. If friendship was uppermost in Washington's mind, there is good evidence that Martha felt more than a few romantic flutterings. Her first husband had been twenty years older than she—and towering, handsome Colonel Washington must have been a breathtaking sight in his full-dress military uniform. To the end of her life, Martha saved a piece of her wedding dress—white brocaded satin threaded with silver—and the white military gloves her tall colonel wore as he took her hand in marriage.

4

A New Life

FOR THE NEXT SIXTEEN YEARS, from 1759 to 1775, Washington was content to be George Washington, Esquire, master of Mount Vernon.

"I am now, I believe," he wrote to a cousin in England, "fixed at this seat with an agreeable consort for life. And I hope to find more happiness in retirement than I ever experienced amidst the wide and bustling world." For most of these sixteen years Sally Fairfax and her husband were at Belvoir. The two couples saw each other constantly. In Washington's cryptic journal there are innumerable references to "dinner with Mr. and Mrs. Fairfax," "dined at Belvoir." But there is not a hint of that passionate longing that Washington exposed to Sally only a few months before his marriage. Could there be better proof that he had achieved his goal of self-mastery?

There was also a vast amount of work to occupy him. Martha's estate involved thousands of acres of land, more than a hundred thousand dollars in cash, and Bank of England bonds. There were legal tangles to be unraveled, farms to be reorganized and supervised. Mount Vernon itself was showing woeful signs of neglect. Washington soon acquired the habit of rising at four A.M. to handle correspondence and keep his account books in order.

This was only one of a dozen ways in which he demonstrated that it was almost impossible for him to do anything in an unexceptional manner. He soon proved to be one of the best businessmen and most original farmers in America. The standard farm crop in Virginia was tobacco; plantations only raised corn and wheat for food and as a sideline. Washington became convinced that the whole procedure was uneconomical. He bought from England the latest books on agricultural science and soon completely revolutionized Mount Vernon's operations. Instead of tobacco, he raised wheat, establishing his own mill in the bargain; before long the Mount Vernon trademark was selling briskly on the local market.

No one in Virginia raised sheep. Washington did, convinced that they were the most profitable animal. He denounced the Virginia habit of exhausting the soil and then letting it lie fallow. It offended his passion for quality, efficiency. He wrote one of his farm managers: "My object is to labor for profit, and therefore to regard quality, instead of quantity, there being . . . no difference between attending a good plant and an indifferent one."

Washington never worshipped any technique simply because it was the prevailing mode. He designed a many-sided barn in which 30 laborers could thresh wheat, instead of letting horses tread it in the open, where weather frequently damaged it. He experimented with breeding mules, convinced they were much better—and cheaper—farm animals than horses. He devoted much attention to trying to develop a domesticated variety of the American wild grape, with which to begin a native wine industry. He established fisheries along his riverbanks and caught thousands of pounds of herring and shad. In later years he opened a distillery at Mount Vernon, where whiskey was made from "rye chiefly and Indian corn in a certain proportion."

When one considers that on Mount Vernon alone, Washington was supervising the operations of more than three hundred people, and that the Custis farms involved perhaps twice this number, the extent of his responsibility becomes impressive. He was years ahead of his time in his approach to the job. Eighteenth-century America was in love with an Arcadian ideal, where every man was his own boss and the first freedom was the right to loaf. Washington's energy clashed head on with this attitude. He berated carpenters who took as much as seven weeks to build a gate for a pasture fence. He was constantly on his horse, checking up on overseers' reports. "System," he declared, "is essential to carry on business well, and with ease."

Mount Vernon was divided into five farms; each had an overseer who made a weekly written report accounting for the time of every worker on the farm. Periodic reports on the livestock were also required. Always, Washington struggled to get that first requirement of a realistic man, an accurate accounting. When the Mount Vernon blacksmith did work for a farm, Washington insisted that the smith charge for each job as accurately as if it were for an outsider.

How well did Washington succeed as a businessman? Although land he inherited from his father and brother, plus more land and cash from his wife's estate, gave him a good start, his skillful management constantly increased the value of this inheritance. When Washington died, Mount Vernon itself had grown to 9,000 acres—13 square miles. He owned a total of 23,000 acres and estimated his net worth at half a million dollars. His heirs, disputing his rock bottom figures, placed it well over a million. Washington achieved this fortune while spending twenty-one of his adult years in public service away from Mount Vernon.

He was no less successful with the estates of Martha's children, which were his responsibility. When Jack Custis reached his majority, he found himself one of the richest young men in Virginia, with a patrimony that had more than doubled under Washington's intensive care.

During these years, Washington's duties as a member of Virginia's House of Burgesses also absorbed some of his time. He was elected shortly before his marriage and took his seat on his twenty-seventh birthday. A few days later a fellow Burgess offered the following resolution: ''That the thanks of the House be given to George Washington, Esquire, late Colonel of the First Virginia Regiment, for his faithful services to His Majesty and this colony and for his brave and steady behavior from the first encroachments and hostilities to the French and their Indians to his resignation after the happy reduction of Fort Duquesne.''

The resolution was passed immediately with a roar of ayes. According to tradition, Washington, rising to acknowledge it, blushed, stammered,

On January 6, 1759, Washington married Martha Dandridge Custis, a wealthy young widow with two children. George and Martha would have no children of their own.

and found himself completely unable to say a word. "Sit down, Mr. Washington," said Speaker Robinson, "your modesty is equal to your valor and that surpasses the power of any language that I possess."

For fifteen years Washington faithfully attended the meetings of this assembly. They were the golden age of Virginia's colonial government. Patrick Henry and Thomas Jefferson were among the great names who debated the political issues of the day. Washington, the realist, had no pretensions about his oratorical abilities. Recalling him, Thomas Jefferson later said, "I served with General Washington in the legislature of Virginia before the revolution and during it with Dr. Franklin in Congress. I never heard either of them speak ten minutes at a time nor to any but the main point which was to decide the question. They laid their shoulders to the great points, knowing that the little ones would follow of themselves.''

That Washington knew what he was doing was evident from a letter of later years when one of his favorite nephews was elected a Burgess and made a well-thought-of speech in his first attempt. ''You have, I find, broke the ice,'' Washington wrote to him. ''The only advice I will offer to you on the occasion (if you have mind to command the attention of the House) is to speak seldom but to important subjects . . .''

Marriage to Martha brought with it the responsibilities of parenthood. Washington became the stepfather of Jack Custis, aged six, and Patsy Custis, aged four. (Martha's other two children had died.) In the first order of goods shipped to him from London after his marriage, Washington ordered ''ten shillings worth of toys,'' ''six little books for children beginning to read,'' and ''one fashionable dressed baby [doll] to cost ten shillings.'' The children called Washington ''Poppa'' and were as fond of him as he was of them. As a boy, Jack Custis signed his letters to him ''Your most affectionate and dutiful son.''

The daughter, Patsy, was the source of much

grief to the Washingtons. As she grew older she developed a form of epilepsy. Washington consulted the best doctors he could find, paying fees of well over 100 dollars for their useless advice. Nothing helped Patsy, and she died in the midst of a seizure in 1773 at the age of sixteen.

How deeply Washington felt her death can be seen from his letter to Martha's relatives telling them of the loss of "our dear Patsy Custis . . . The sweet innocent girl entered into a more happy and peaceful abode than any she has met with in the afflicted path she hitherto has trod. This sudden and unexpected blow, I scare need add, has almost reduced my poor wife to the lowest ebb of misery."

From the beginning of their marriage, Washington struggled in vain to cope with Martha's overwhelming anxiety for her children. Perhaps because of Patsy's illness, she was a compulsively doting mother and made it difficult, if not impossible, for Washington to give Jack Custis the kind of upbringing his stepfather felt he needed. Washington was determined, as he wrote to one tutor, to make him "fit for more useful purposes than a horse racer." He was almost pathetically anxious to give the boy the education he himself had failed to get. Martha's indulgence and Jack's temperament made it a losing battle from the start. By the time Jack was fourteen, Washington was writing to a tutor that "his mind is . . . more turned to dogs, horses, and guns, indeed upon dress and equipage." Soon Jack's tutor was reporting a more alarming development—" a propensity for the fair sex." At nineteen, without telling either his mother or his stepfather, Jack engaged himself to an Annapolis belle named Nellie Calvert.

Washington pleaded successfully with the young couple to put off marriage so Jack could complete his education. He then hustled Jack to New York, where he personally enrolled him in Kings College (later Columbia) for what he hoped would be two years of hard study. When Patsy Custis died only a month later, Martha could not endure having her only remaining child so far away from her. Jack was permitted to return, and he promptly married dark-eyed Nellie while Washington watched in silent frustration.

Where another man might have blamed the boy for so resolutely refusing his advice, Washington never seemed to have held the slightest grudge against him. He was soon writing to "Dear Jack," urging him and Nellie to visit Mount Vernon as often as possible.

Washington had a lifelong fondness for children. One woman, Mrs. John M. Bowers, preserved to the end of her days the memory of the time when as a child she was taken to visit Washington, by then old and famous, and he sat her on his knee and sang to her.

After one of the most disastrous of his Revolutionary War battles, he stopped for the night at a farmhouse, and a little girl begged and begged to see him. Finally her mother summoned the nerve to ask the exhausted Washington, who simply nodded. The wide-eyed youngster was brought in and Washington took her in his lap and said, "Well, my dear, you see a very tired man in a *very* dirty shirt."

Another time, during a wartime trip with the French volunteer Mathieu Dumas, a great crowd of children greeted Washington as he approached the town of Providence. Washington stopped and returned their greeting, then turned to Dumas and, pressing his hand, said, "We may be beaten by the English; it is the chance of war; but behold an army which they can never conquer."

In 1783, after he resigned his commission as commander-in-chief and rode home to Mount Vernon, the conqueror of a continent and First Citizen of the world, he had the following items in his saddlebags, purchased as Christmas presents for Martha's grandchildren:

A locket   5 5

3 small pocketbooks   1 10 shillings

Children's books   4 shillings 6 pence
Whilagig   1 shilling 6 pence
Fiddle   2 shillings 6 pence
Quadrile boxes   1 pound 17 shillings 6 pence

His easygoing ways with Jack Custis were typical of Washington's relations with all those he
called "his kin." To his brother Augustine he
wrote, "The pleasure of your company at Mount
Vernon always did and always will afford me
infinite satisfaction," and signed himself "your
most affectionate brother." His second and favorite brother, Jack, Washington described as "the
intimate companion of my youth and the friend
of my ripened age." In his will, Washington left
Mount Vernon to Jack's son Bushrod. With his
brother Samuel, closest to Washington in age,
and his youngest brother Charles, there was not
as much warmth but Washington never hesitated
to lend them money when they needed it, which
was often. Samuel inherited none of Washington's financial ability and was constantly in
debt. Charles died an alcoholic.

Washington was equally fond of his in-laws.
He was constantly visiting back and forth with
Burwell Basset, married to Martha's sister, and
Fielding Lewis, husband of his own sister Betty.
He did not even have the traditional antipathy to

his mother-in-law. After Patsy's death, he wrote the Bassets that he "wished he was master of arguments powerful enough" to persuade Martha's mother, Mrs. Dandridge, to make Mount Vernon "her entire and absolute home." He was, of course, hoping her presence would aid Martha in her grief.

Only with his mother did Washington continue to have a strained or, at best, distant, relationship. He was a dutiful son, going to Fredericksburg whenever she summoned him, supervising the operation of her plantation, and giving her money whenever she requested it. Mary Ball was not satisfied with his respectful service. She seems to have been perpetually resentful that she never succeeded in dominating her oldest son. She expressed her disappointment with endless complaints about her wants and needs. Eventually, she became so grasping that Washington was forced to call in his brother Charles as a witness every time he gave her money and to keep a careful record of each gift so she could not slander him with the rest of the family.

With his relatives and friends, the Washington of these years began a lifetime habit of secret generosity. He wrote to William Ramsey, for whom he had worked as a surveyor in Alexandria, and asked him if he would permit him to send his son, who, Washington understood, was "a youth fond of study and instruction" to "the Jersey College" (now Princeton). "No other return is expected or wished for this offer," Washington vowed, "than that you will accept it with the same freedom and good will with which it is made, and that you may not even consider it in the light of an obligation or mention it as such; for be assured that from me it will never be known."

When Billy Fairfax, younger brother of his close friend George, bought a commission in the Royal Army, Washington sent him 50 pounds, telling him he did not care whether it was repaid this year, next year, or in seven years. Poor Billy probably never did repay it; he died not long after, fighting under Wolfe on the Plains of Abraham in the battle that won Canada.

In later years, Washington shouldered the burden of educating and otherwise supporting twenty-two nieces and nephews. On two boys alone, sons of his brother Samuel, he at one time estimated he had spent more than 5,000 dollars. During his Presidency, the tangled state of the nation's finances left Washington extremely short of cash. Yet every Christmas he gave, always in secret, at least 250 dollars, sometimes as much as 500 dollars to charity. An artist who had taught drawing at Mount Vernon, and knew his man well, wrote once asking for 80 dollars. ''I prefer to owe you that favor than to anybody else, being certain of secrecy.'' He got his money.

The sharp temper and combativeness of the warrior could still flare up, especially when a man for whom Washington had small regard nettled him. An ex-officer, George Muse, who had been cashiered for cowardice in the battle at Fort Necessity, accused Washington of trying to cheat him out of his share of the western bounty lands, which the government had voted the soldiers of that unfortunate expedition. Washington's reply was the epitome of verbal destruction.

Sir, Your impertinent letter was delivered to me yesterday. As I am not accustomed to receiving such from any man nor would have taken the same language from you personally without letting you feel some marks of my resentment. I advise you to be cautious in writing me a second of the same tenor; for I understand you were drunk when you did it, yet give me leave to tell you that drunkenness is no excuse for rudeness. But for your stupidity and sottishness you might have known by attending to the public gazette that you had your full quantity of ten thousand acres of land allowed you . . . but suppose you had really fallen short, do you think your superlative merit entitles you to greater indulgence than others, or if it did that I was to make it good to you? . . . All my concern is

that I ever engaged myself in behalf of so ungrate-
ful and dirty a fellow as you are.

Another time, Washington was riding across
his Mount Vernon acres when he heard the sound
of a gun. Riding swiftly toward it, he heard another shot and saw a duck plummeting into the
water along the Potomac shore. Crouched in a
canoe among the reeds was a familiar figure from
across the river, a poacher whom Washington had
ordered off his land at least twice. With a shout of
rage Washington sent his horse thundering down
the riverbank into the water and through the
bushes at this well-warned thief. The poacher
leaped up, aimed his gun at Washington, and
screamed, "Stop or I shoot." Totally ignoring the
threat, Washington leaned from his horse, seized
the prow of the canoe, and dragged craft and
passenger back to land. There Washington sprang
to the ground and thrashed the gunnman until he
swore on his knees never to trespass on Mount
Vernon again.

These were only interludes. Most of his years
at Mount Vernon were rich in peace and pleasure
for Washington. Just as he was no unrelenting
moralist with Jack Custis or any of his kin, he was
no puritan with himself. When he went to Fredericksburg he spent many happy evenings at

George Weedon's Indian Queen Tavern, where men of military inclination gathered. An often-repeated local tradition tells of the night a British officer sang a song "as funny as it was improper," which caused Washington to laugh until tears ran down his cheeks and call upon the singer for an encore. It was here, too, according to his account books, that he once won 30 guineas at cards. Tradition maintains this—if ever—was the night he threw his historic coin across the Rappahannock.

A story from these happy Mount Vernon days confirms the possibility, at least. A group of young men were "throwing the bar"—a popular sport of the time. A heavy iron bar was whirled, somewhat in the manner of a modern discus throw, with the prize going to the man who sent it farthest. The forty-year-old Washington happened to stroll past, and someone asked him if he wanted a chance to see if his arm still retained any of its youthful oomph. He promptly doffed his coat, seized the bar, and sent it flying a good dozen yards beyond the best toss of the day.

Washington may well have won a few dollars on the throw. He always enjoyed a friendly bet. Cards were high on his list of favorite games. The stakes were never extravagant but they were sometimes high enough. One night he lost more than 70 dollars. He also loved a good horse race and bet on them frequently, losing (as he did at cards) about as often as he won. Lotteries were also popular in Virginia at the time, and whenever tickets were hawked the master of Mount Vernon was a ready customer. The theater was another of his favorite recreations. He rarely went to Williamsburg without seeing a play.

Even more than the theater he loved a dance. He was always ready to help organize one and would ride ten or twenty miles to attend one. His surplus energy found a ready outlet on the dance floor. More than once he was known to whirl away a whole night and quit only when the musicians collapsed at dawn.

The only other pastime that equalled his fondness for dancing was fox hunting. Here the martial spirit of the man, his innate love of excitement and danger got full play. He rode a huge fiery horse named Blueskin which, like all his horses, he had broken himself. As huntsman he had a mulatto slave named Billy Lee, who was at least as daring and skillful as he was. Lee's orders were simple: at all costs he was to "keep with the hounds." Invariably Washington was right behind him, hurtling at breakneck speed over fences and through tangled woods. On his own

Mount Vernon property there were paths cut through the trees by which more timid riders could follow the hunt with less risk to life and limb. No one ever saw Washington take one of these paths. A glimpse of the passion with which he pursued the fox can be obtained from his diaries for six typical years, January, 1768 to March, 1774. In this span he went fox hunting 155 times. He gunned, usually for duck, only 31 times, and fished almost not at all, only 5 times.

He was notably fond of his horses and dogs, especially one French hound, named "Old Vulcan." Once this favorite stole a ham just cooked for some guests. Martha was indignant, but Washington thought it was funny and told his guests that they would have to take pot luck since Vulcan had just eaten their dinner.

A man who lived such a sociable existence inevitably dressed for it. Washington was never slow to spend his money for good clothes. His favorite word when ordering goods from London was "fashionable." He was, on the other hand, no dude. "I want neither lace nor embroidery," he wrote to his agent. "Plain clothes with a gold or silver button . . . are all I desire." In another letter he made it clear he wanted the best, ordering "a genteel suit of clothes made of superfine broadcloth, handsomely chosen." When his carriage collapsed, he ordered a replacement from England ''in the newest taste, handsome, genteel and light . . . to be made of the best seasoned wood and by a celebrated workman.'' He wanted it painted green ''unless any other color more in vogue and equally lasting is entitled to precedency.'' On its doors he had engraved the Washington coat of arms.

He enjoyed good wine, ordering it by the ''pipe''—110-gallon kegs. After dinner, he liked to sit around the table, drinking numerous toasts and sampling a dish of nuts, of which he was equally fond. After all his years of glory, he said, ''I had rather be at Mount Vernon with a friend or two about me than to be attended at the seat of government by the officers of state and the representatives of every power in Europe.''

In these later years, when his house was constantly thronged with visitors from all over the world, eager to see George Washington, the great man, he sighed that Mount Vernon had become merely ''a well restored tavern.'' In 1796, he noted in his diary, that ''Mrs. Washington and myself sat down to dinner alone tonight for the first time in twenty years.''

Because he did not slap the back of every curiosity seeker who shook his hand, Washington was accused of being cold and formal by many of these visitors. He could not explain he had a vast estate to supervise; he simply went about his business. Strangers were often startled to meet him in his working clothes. One broiling summer day, a visitor asked where he might find the "General." A member of the family pointed the stranger in the right direction and said, "You will meet, sir, with an old gentleman riding alone, in plain drab clothes, a broad brimmed white hat, a hickory switch in his hand, and carrying an umbrella with a long staff, which is attached to his saddlebow—that person, sir, is General Washington."

Hard as he worked and played in Virginia, Washington remained stirred by the vast continent he had seen beyond the western mountains. He represented the soldiers of his old regiment in the often-delicate negotiations for the 200,000 bounty acres promised them for their services on the frontier. When the lands were finally granted, Washington eagerly bought up the portions of those who did not care to go west to stake out their claims.

This western vision, like his love of innovation and experiment, is part of the little-known Washington who foresaw so much in American history. His idea of the West deepened and grew throughout his life until he was writing in later years: "The Western country promises to afford a capacious asylum for the poor and persecuted of the earth."

In 1769, Washington and Dr. James Craik, who had been the surgeon of the Virginia regiment and remained one of Washington's closest friends, took a seven-week trip through the Ohio country to appraise the value of the various tracts. Along the route they met an Indian chief who had fought on the French side at Braddock's defeat. The chief said he clearly remembered Washington's huge frame as he rode about the battlefield on that terrible day:

> I called to my young men and said, "Mark yon tall and daring warrior." Our rifles were levelled, rifles which but for him knew not how to miss—'twas all in vain. A power mightier far than we shielded him from harm. He cannot die in battle. I am old and soon shall be gathered to the great council fire of my fathers in the land of shades, but ere I go there is something bids me speak in the voice of prophesy. Listen! The great spirit protects that man and guides his destinies—he will become the chief of nations and a people yet unborn will hail him as the founder of a mighty empire.

The wording is, of course, Dr. Craik's recollection. The experience made a lasting impression on the doctor's mind. He was to tell this story repeatedly in coming decades. Characteristically, Washington did not even note it in his diary. As an old Indian hand, he was familiar with the extravagant flattery chiefs were inclined to bestow on anyone they considered important. As a realist, the idea that he, an obscure Virginia colonel who never even managed to get a Royal commission, was destined to found a nation, must have struck him as nonsense that only the liquor-fired imagination of an ignorant Indian could concoct.

However, there had already been rumblings of trouble between England and her colonies. In 1765, Washington had sat in the House of Burgesses and heard Patrick Henry utter his famous cry, ''Caesar had his Brutus, Charles I his Cromwell, and George III may profit by their example. If this be treason, make the most of it.''

In 1769, when Parliament tried once more to tax the recalcitrant colonies, Patrick Henry and numerous others made more speeches. Washington did something more practical. He got on his horse and personally persuaded some one thousand Virginians to sign a solemn pledge not to import any item from England on which Parliament had levied a tax. A letter to his neighbor George Mason offers remarkable evidence that while other men talked of appeals and embargoes, Washington's ever realistic eyes saw, six years before the event, that the final test of strength would be on the battlefield.

> At a time when our lordly masters in Great Britian will be satisfied with nothing less than the deprivation of American freedom, it seems highly necessary that something should be done to avert the stroke and maintain the liberty which we have derived from our ancestors . . . that no man should scruple or hesitate a moment to use a-ms in defense of so valuable a blessing on which all the good and evil of life depends is clearly my opinion. Yet a-ms, I would beg leave to add, should be the last resource, the dernier resort.

In the next four years, the British Parliament staggered from folly to folly, repealing one tax and imposing another, confessing, on the one hand, it did not have the power to enforce its will on the colonies and refusing, on the other hand, to concede or modify that power. Washington watched the performance and saw nothing that made him change his opinion. Yet his best friends, the Fairfaxes, disagreed strongly with him. Though they sympathized with the Americans, their ties to England were much too close to contemplate breaking them. In 1773, George William and Sally Fairfax decided to go to England to supervise the Fairfax interests there and protect George William's claim to the family title.

From 1759 to 1774, Washington lived a quiet life at Mount Vernon and the Custis farms, working and hunting the land.

On the afternoon before they sailed, they made a last trip to Mount Vernon to say good-bye to the Washingtons; and on the day itself, George and Martha rode to Belvoir "to see them take shipping." It was his last glimpse of that unattainable woman he had loved as a youth. Events were sweeping Sally and Washington into a cataclysm that would forever alter both their lives.

5

In Search of an Army

WITHIN A FEW MONTHS there was more trouble with England. The tax on tea, symbol of Parliament's determination to retain its power, was answered by a band of Bostonians, disguised as Mohawk Indians, who dumped 350 chests of Washington's favorite beverage into Boston harbor. Parliament's response was to shut the port of Boston and impose martial law. When the Virginia Assembly attempted to pass a resolution supporting Boston, the Royal Governor dissolved it. Twenty-five Burgesses, including Washington, met privately and decided to call a meeting of the Assembly independently of the Governor.

During these same troubled weeks, Washington argued what was at stake in an exchange of letters with Bryan Fairfax, brother of George William and an equally close friend. There is something hauntingly symbolic about this correspondence with a man whose name summed up the greatness and glory of the England Washington had learned to worship in his youth.

"I think myself bound to oppose violent measures now," wrote Fairfax.

"I would heartily join you," returned Washington, ". . . provided there was the most distant hope of success. But have we not . . . addressed the lords and remonstrated to the Commons? And to what end?"

"You have no reason to doubt your own opinion," returns Bryan Fairfax. "It is I that have reason to doubt mine when so many men of superior understanding think otherwise."

"I've scarce passed a day without anxious thoughts on the subject," said Washington. "I beg leave to look upon you as a friend and it is a great relief to unbosom one's thoughts to a friend, for I am convinced no man in the colony wishes its prosperity more, would go to greater lengths to serve it, nor is there at the same time a better subject of the Crown."

Never, when he could help it, did Washington let a difference of opinion destroy a friendship. But his own mind was made up. On August 1st, at the meeting of the Virginia Assembly in Williamsburg, he arose and in a one-sentence speech completely stole the show from Patrick

Henry and his fellow orators. "I am ready to raise one thousand men," he said, "subsist them myself at my own expense and march at their head to Boston."

As a result, Washington was the third of seven Virginians chosen to represent the colony in the first Continental Congress. When we consider the array of orators and politicians and political thinkers of first rank against whom he was competing, the choice is a remarkable testimony to the magnetism which this big, normally silent, man exercised on his contemporaries.

In the Congress's seven weeks of speech-making and debate, George Washington never made a public statement; but he played a powerful role in the long nightly conversations after the public sessions. Patrick Henry, when asked whom he considered the greatest man in Congress, answered, "Rutledge if you speak of eloquence is by far the greatest orator, but Colonel Washington, who has no pretensions to eloquence, is a man of more solid judgment and information than any man on that floor."

Washington heard the news of the bloodshed at Lexington shortly before he was reelected a delegate to the second Continental Congress. When he took his place at this historic convention, he wore his blue and buff uniform of the

Virginia militia. It was, again, a typically Wash-
ingtonian bit of silent eloquence. Shrewd New
Englanders, like John Adams, quickly saw that
they needed a southerner to lead the largely
Yankee army that had gathered outside British-
occupied Boston. There were several contenders
besides Washington, two former British officers—
Horatio Gates and Charles Lee—and John Hancock, the Congress president.

In his diary, John Adams recalled the moment
when he arose to nominate Washington as
commander-in-chief. With superb tact, Washington immediately slipped out a side door so
that no one need hesitate to speak frankly on his
suitability. As for John Hancock, Adams, watching his face as he spoke, recalled, ''I never remarked a more sudden and striking change of
countenance. Mortification and resentment were
expressed as forcibly as his face could exhibit
them.'' It was a hint of things to come. A well
organized minority of New Englanders strongly
resented Washington's elevation.

A few days later, when a final vote was taken
and the command was formally offered to him,
Washington rose and made a brief speech. It was,
typically, lacking in eloquence. It had no high-
flown phrases about liberty and the rights of
man. Instead it was very personal, indirectly re-

vealing how deeply the offer touched Washington's strongest emotions. Here was that "title of honor" he had pursued, in Lawrence's name, across the western mountains, offered to him, not at the pleasure of a monarch, but as the gift of a free people.

What was Washington's first reaction? Not joy or happiness. Only the gravity of the all-to-realistic truth: he might fail. He knew he was going forth to challenge the mightiest nation in the world, Imperial Britain, whose fleets and armies dominated the globe. He had never commanded anything larger than a regiment. After thanking Congress for the "high honour," Washington said, "I feel great distress from a consciousness that my abilities and Military experience may not be equal to the extensive and important trust . . . I beg it may be remembered by every gentleman in the room that I this day declare with the utmost sincerity I do not think myself equal to the command."

In this touchingly simple statement, Washington created one of the hallmarks of his greatness. He did not ride into history like an Alexander or a Napoleon, trumpeting his military genius. He did not see himself as a superman. He knew from harsh experience that defeat was all too possible. All he offered was a vow to "exert every power I possess . . . for the support of the glorious cause.''

As for pay, Washington refused it. No amount of money, he told the Congress, ''could have tempted me to accept this arduous employment at the expense of my domestic ease and happiness.'' All he asked was reimbursement of his expenses.

The momentous duty accepted, Washington's first thought was of Martha. He wrote to ''My dear Patsy'' [his affectionate name for Martha] words that underline the sincerity of his speech to the Continental Congress.

> You may believe me when I assure you in the most solemn manner that so far from seeking this appointment, I have used every endeavor in my power to avoid it, not only from my unwillingness to part with you and the family but from a consciousness of its being a trust too great for my capacity . . . It was utterly out of my power to refuse . . . without exposing my character to such censures as would have reflected dishonor upon myself and given pain to my friends.

He also wrote to his favorite brother, Jack. ''I am now to bid adieu to you and every kind of domestic ease for awhile. I am embarked on a wide ocean, boundless in its prospect and in which perhaps no safe harbor is to be found.'' He urged Jack to visit Martha often. "My departure will, I know, be a cutting stroke upon her; and on this account alone I have many disagreeable sensations."

On the 23rd of June he rode north to take command of the American army before Boston. His farewell letter to Martha suggests that over the years she had come a long way toward replacing Sally Fairfax in Washington's heart. "I would not think of departing . . . without dropping you a line," he wrote. "I return an unalterable affection for you which neither time nor distance can change."

With those words, George Washington, the Virginia gentleman, turned his back on the past and rode into an American future. But he did not become American overnight.

6

In Search of a Country

FOR THE FIRST FEW MONTHS there was much in Washington's correspondence that suggested that the hypersensitive young Virginia colonel had not been outgrown. He took a very dim view of New Englanders as soldiers. "They regard their officers as no more than broomsticks," he moaned. The officers, in Washington's opinion, were not much better. He dressed down a Connecticut captain of horse whom he caught shaving a private soldier on the parade ground just outside headquarters. He severely reprimanded a lieutenant for "infamous conduct and degrading himself by voluntarily doing the duty of an orderly sergeant." Soon he was describing New Englanders in general as "a dirty and nasty people animated by a dirty mercenary spirit."

Suddenly there was a change. Some people think it may have come from the worst of the numerous shocks he received in the months after he took command of the chaotic army. (It took him more than a week to find out how many men he had; instead of the estimated 20,000, there were really 14,000.) Now into headquarters rushed a member of his staff to inform him that there had been a miscount of the power barrels. Instead of a reserve of 485, there were 38. The old George Washington would have exploded in tumultuous rage. This was a man who at 43 was still growing. General John Sullivan, who was there, always remembered Washington's reaction: silence. "He was so struck he did not utter a word for a half hour," Sullivan said.

Thereafter there was a steady decline of sectional criticism in Washington's letters until it finally vanished completely. In that silent half hour he apparently took stock of himself and the people he was trying to lead, and with his profound realism saw that neither was prepared to fight the British Empire for possession of a continent. Their one hope of succeeding was unity: to become neither Massachusetts men nor Connecticut men, neither New Yorkers nor Virginians, but Americans.

With that inner decision, George Washington set himself to the task of simultaneously defending and creating an America that did not yet exist.

The problems were staggering. His 14,000 men

were more mob than army. Discipline, particularly among the independent New Englanders, was a dirty word. Worse, officers resigned by the dozen in squabbles over seniority or rank. Washington had to spend endless hours soothing wounded egos and writing Congress for permission to juggle commissions and fill vacancies. He had to reduce the regiments to a uniform size and retain the best officers. This involved him in violent interstate rivalries.

"Connecticut wants no Massachusetts man in their corps; Massachusetts thinks there is no necessity for Rhode Island men to be introduced among them; and New Hampshire says it's very hard that her valuable and experienced officers should be discarded . . ." The Governor of Maryland said he wanted permission for his troops to remain in their home state. His friend George Mason wrote, warning him that Virginia would go bankrupt if it tried to raise 3,000 men. There was a plan to invade Canada, a need to fortify New York. The frontier was trembling at the prospect of a British-led Indian war.

Washington had to grapple with such vast strategic questions and simultaneously try to mold an army—while nine thousand British professional soldiers were poised to attack from fortified Boston the moment they saw signs of American weakness.

Strategy, diplomacy, supplies, organization, America needed all of these things. Only a fighting army would win a war, and only a general capable of controlling the unruly headstrong Americans of 1776 could lead such an army. Washington soon proved he was the man.

A snowball fight between the soldiers of the Marblehead regiment and Morgan's Virginia riflemen turned into a riot which soon had a thousand men in full mutiny against their officers, punching and kicking each other in the snow. The colonel of the Marblehead regiment rushed to Washington's headquarters with the news. Washington threw himself into the saddle of his horse, always kept at the door, and galloped to the pasture where the troops were battling.

One of his servants, Pompey, had been ordered ahead to take down the pasture bars, but Washington was on top of him before he could do the job. Without so much as a pause in his headlong rush, Washington sent his horse soaring over Pompey and the bars into the midst of the rioters. Leaping from the saddle, he grabbed two brawny soldiers by the throats and lifted them off the ground, one in each hand, shaking them like children while he roared commands at the rest, which instantly extinguished the fight.

John Sullivan, who witnessed this scene, later said, ''From the moment I saw Washington leap the bars at Cambridge and realized his personal ascendency over the turbulent tempers of his men in their moments of wildest excitement, I never faltered in the faith that we had the right man to lead the cause of American liberty.''

Washington's innate gifts for leadership were all but hamstrung by the Continental Congress. The politicians reserved to themselves the right to appoint all of Washington's general officers. The states reserved the right to appoint all the junior officers up to the rank of colonel. When Washington asked for an army of 50,000 men with long-term, preferably three-year, enlistments, Congress brushed him off. There was a deep fear that establishment of a standing army would lead to a military dictatorship. As a result, much of Washington's energies were consumed frantically trying to recruit a new army to replace the one that was dissolving in front of his eyes as three- and six-month recruits picked up their guns and went home.

Overwhelmed by paper work, Washington was equally frantic to find qualified staff officers. It is amazing how many men of ability and talent saw not the slightest need to volunteer their services. Twenty-six signers of the Declaration of Independence were younger than Washington; not one volunteered. Bravos like Patrick Henry resigned because they were not made generals. When the grandson of the wealthy Virginian Landon Carter refused a commission because his mother objected, Washington wrote ruefully to his father, "A mother's tenderness and tears too often interpose a check on the ardor of our youth." He could have said he had overcome the same check in his youth, but it never occurred to Washington to hold himself up as an example.

Over the course of the war Washington lost no less than eighteen generals through resignation or court martial. At least a half dozen others resigned and were cajoled back by their commander-in-chief. Only with fellow Virginians did Washington demand as much as he asked of himself. When Colonel Theodorick Bland asked to resign, pleading financial distress, Washington told him that a man such as he must remain with the army "at the cost of private affairs."

For a full year Washington begged and pleaded for a better military policy, and Congress did nothing. Thus he went into battle in the summer of 1776 with a partially trained army of little more than 9,000 men, which he had to enlarge with totally amateur militiamen fresh from the farms, for a month or two months service. Against him were pitted 32,000 superbly equipped and disciplined British soldiers. Small wonder that the year 1776 brought a series of shocking disasters for the American cause. Not even a Washington could cope with troops like the two brigades of Connecticut militia, who fled from their trenches at New York's Kips Bay before an advance guard of 100 British light infantry.

Kips Bay was, in many ways, the worst hour of Washington's life. We have seen, again and again, how this man of tumultuous emotion achieved self-mastery by enormous effort. The awful sight of 4,000 Americans in headlong flight from a handful of British momentarily annihilated this achievement. In a fury, he flung his hat on the ground and cried out, "Are these the men I am to defend America with?" Cursing like a man possessed, he flailed officers and men with a cane-whip. Nothing stopped the raw panic that swept these amateur soldiers past him like a stampede of wild animals. Finally, Washington was left alone on the field, within a hundred yards of the British advance guard.

He sat there on his horse, numb with rage and disgust, almost asking them to kill him. Fortunately, the British soldiers were baffled by the sight of an unguarded American general and hesitated, suspecting a trap. An aide rode up, seized Washington's bridle, and led his horse away. Thomas Jefferson, who saw Washington fly into a similar rage when he was President, reported that the paroxysm left him in the same dazed, incoherent state. There was, indeed, a primitive man beneath that usually serene exterior. The intuitive Indians named him well when they called him *Conotocarious*.

There were only a few things that could evoke this raging primitive in Washington. One of them was cowardice. He was so totally fearless in battle himself that he was almost incapable of understanding it in other men. He could be harsh, even cruel, with a man who showed so much as a trace of it. At the battle of Long Island, he strode up and down behind the American entrenchments with two pistols in his belt, vowing to shoot the first man he saw running.

At Princeton, in the midst of the battle, he ordered a captain of the Massachusetts line to chop down a bridge across a key river before the oncoming British captured it. The captain nervously surveyed the situation and said, "Are there enough men?"

"Enough to be cut to pieces," Washington roared at him.

According to the story, the captain turned so white that as he rejoined his troops he pinched his cheeks to restore their color lest his men detect his panic and refuse to obey him.

Washington never ceased struggling to control this ferocity, and to an amazing degree, he succeeded. He had a larger motive now—not merely the personal satisfaction of self-mastery—but the imperative need to create a united America. Nothing illustrates his achievement better than his treatment of his close friend and aide, Joseph Reed. One of Philadelphia's most distinguished citizens, Reed quickly became Washington's favorite staff officer. Washington freely wrote him personal opinions about Congress, the quality of his troops, and other matters he would have mentioned only to a man he trusted implicitly.

In the black winter of 1776, as the American army reeled across New Jersey with the British in hot pursuit, Washington opened a letter addressed to Reed, from Major General Charles Lee. Washington thought it was official business. Instead, it was a snide reply from the ambitious Lee to a letter from Reed in which Reed had obviously criticized Washington.

Most men would have considered such a stab in the back unforgivable. The thin-skinned Washington of earlier years would have castigated Reed for his duplicity. Instead, Washington merely passed the letter on to Reed, explaining how he had opened it by mistake. Reed was mortified and sent in his resignation. Washington refused to accept it. Three months later, after Washington had made him a general of the cavalry, Reed wrote a letter attempting to explain his disloyalty away. Washington's answer deserves to be quoted in full because nothing demonstrates how much the man had grown in his eighteen months as an American leader.

> True it is I felt myself hurt by a certain letter. . . . I was hurt not because I thought my judgment wronged by the expressions contained in it, but because the same sentiments were not communicated immediately to myself. The favorable manner in which your opinions upon all occasions had been received . . . entitled me, I thought, to your advice upon any point in which I appeared to be wanting.

7

"Push Along Old Man"

DOWN DWINDLED THE AMERICAN FORTUNES until Congress fled Philadelphia in raw panic and, abandoning all its pretensions to military knowledge, appointed Washington a virtual dictator. For eight weeks he was on his own with total power to call up troops, issue proclamations, and fight his battles where and when he chose. It is staggering to consider what he accomplished in these eight weeks. At midnight on Christmas Day, 1776, he slashed across the ice-choked Delaware to capture 900 bewildered Hessians in Trenton. When the British sent Lord Cornwallis hustling across New Jersey with an army to contain him, Washington produced another midnight maneuver: an end-run that left Cornwallis staring at an empty American camp while Washington was 20 miles at his rear, annihilating three British regiments at Princeton.

Christmas Day, 1776: Washington and his men cross the ice-clogged Delaware River and move on to capture Trenton, NJ.

In eight weeks Washington recaptured two-thirds of New Jersey for the Revolutionary cause, winning two battles that completely reversed the downward plunge of American morale. At the end of these eight weeks, what did he do? He surrendered his dictatorial powers to Congress and became their obedient servant once more, galled and tormented by their ineptitude and inefficiency, harassed by their intrigues. Few things testify to Washington's greatness more than this calm relinquishment of power he had used so well. History is full of other generals who discovered the efficiency of dictatorship and decided to convert it into a principle of government.

Congress showed its gratitude by promptly naming five new major generals and eighteen brigadiers without consulting Washington or even submitting the list to him before announcing it. It was Washington, of course, who had to bear the brunt of a whole new series of resignations and wrangles.

This subservience to Congress is all the more amazing when we consider Washington's ever-realistic eye. He knew that most of the great names that had adorned the Congress which drew up the Declaration of Independence had long since departed. In a letter to financier Robert Morris he admitted as much. "Indeed, sir," he wrote, "your observations on our want of many principled characters in that respectable Senate are but too well founded in truth . . ."

But in Washington, a first-class mind had been combined with a warrior's nature. He knew what he was fighting for. "An innate spirit of freedom," he had written to Bryan Fairfax, led him to defy England's overbearing arrogance. The moment Congress voted him the special powers, he wrote to Robert Morris, "instead of thinking myself free'd from all civil obligation by this mark of their confidence, I shall constantly bear in mind that as the Sword was the last resort for the preservation of our Liberties, so it ought to be the first thing laid aside, when those Liberties are firmly established."

Americans should never forget it was Washington, the warrior, the fierce and fabulous man on horseback who established these liberties. Only Washington could write the words you have just read (and mean them) and four hours later lead his ragged regiments on another stealthy all-night march (his favorite tactic) to hurl them with a roar of delight at the stunned British before Princeton.

No wonder the army worshipped him. He was never an armchair general, running things several safe miles behind the lines. He always rode to the sound of the guns. Were it not for the testimony of eyewitnesses, many stories about his courage would be simply unbelievable.

During the opening skirmish at Princeton, a British regiment momentarily checked and disorganized the American advance guard. Washington, to teach his men contempt for British marksmanship, rode down the whole front of the British regiment, urging his men to form and fire. As he sat on his horse between them, both sides cut loose with a volley; one of his aides, Colonel John Fitzgerald, was so certain Washington was dead, he covered his face with his hat so that he would not see him fall.

When he looked again, there was the big figure on the huge bay horse, cantering exultantly out of the battle smoke to watch the British break and run before the American charge.

When the British took to their heels, Washington pursued them himself like a veritable cavalryman. He and an aide, Colonel Stephen Moylan, soon got so far ahead of their own army they were almost captured by the retreating enemy. Washington was telling Moylan how he planned to surround the fugitives when Moylan suddenly asked, "But where are your troops?" They looked around and saw they were alone on the road.

After the battle, Washington had to listen to a chorus of protests against his recklessness. Benjamin Harrison wrote to Robert Morris, "Every officer complains of his exposing himself too much." This was to be repeated throughout the war.

Perhaps the most amazing story comes from a British officer, Major John Ferguson. An expert at forest warfare, Ferguson was the best shot in the British army. Before the battle of Brandywine, he was scouting the woods near the American lines. Suddenly, through the trees rode a big man on a bay horse, obviously an American officer. It was Washington, on a scout of his own. Only one other horseman was with him. Completely concealed, Ferguson and his men took dead aim on the rider of the bay horse. As fingers tightened on the triggers, Ferguson suddenly signaled to hold their fire. He said, later, that he could not bring himself to shoot a defenseless man.

Revealing himself for an instant, Ferguson called to the two Americans. Obviously, he was hoping they would try to shoot it out with him, and he could then cut them down with a clear conscience. What happened next amazed Ferguson and must amaze anyone who reads it today. *Washington stopped, looked straight into the muzzle of Ferguson's gun, then turned his back and slowly rode away.* "I could have lodged half a dozen of balls in or about him," said the baffled Ferguson. "But it was not pleasant to fire at the back of an unoffending individual, who was acquitting himself very coolly of his duty, so I let him alone." Only much later did he learn the identity of his target.

At this same battle of Brandywine, Washington and his staff learned, almost too late, that a British column was about to assault the American right flank. In fact, as they heard the news, the crash of cannon and musketry rolled over the hills to them. Washington instantly decided to head for this danger zone. To use the shortest possible route, he commandeered the help of an elderly farmer, one Joseph Brown, who knew the country well. Brown was only a lukewarm patriot and had no enthusiasm for riding to the guns. He made a dozen excuses. Finally, one of Washington's staff leaped from his horse, drew his sword, and while Washington watched with grim approval, the man told Brown if he did not get on his horse and start riding, he would run him through on the spot.

Brown took off on the wildest ride of his life. Over fences and up and down hills he careened. Every pounding hoofbeat of the way, Washington's horse had his nose all but glued to

Brown's flank, while Washington continually growled in the farmer's ear, "Push along, old man. Push along, old man."

There was also a deep humanity in Washington that saved him from the brutal extremes of the soldier's code. He felt no personal animosity toward the British. At Princeton, watching one outnumbered body of redcoats defending itself fiercely against attacking Americans, Washington cried out, "See how those noble fellows fight!" When a battle was over he was generosity itself to prisoners and wounded. At Princeton he found one wounded British soldier being robbed by several American stragglers. Washington angrily drove the Americans away and ordered another man to stand guard over the bleeding redcoat until American doctors arrived to help him.

Nor did he send men to their deaths without a pang. Watching vastly outnumbered Marylanders launch a doomed assault on a horde of British at Long Island, he cried out, "My God, what brave fellows I must lose this day!" During the retreat across New Jersey, Daniel Neil was one of the few local militiamen who volunteered to join Washington. An artilleryman, Neil was killed fighting at Princeton, leaving a widow and two small children. The desperate woman, faced with starvation, wrote Washington for help. He forwarded her letter to the Continental Congress, who forthwith informed him that there was no provision for widows of soldiers—though the war had gone on now for two years. Washington regretfully informed Mrs. Neil of Congress's position, and enclosed with his letter 50 dollars of his own money.

Americans in British hands were among Washington's major concerns. For months he searched desperately for a man who would take the difficult job of Commissary of Prisoners. Finally, in April, 1777, he approached a capable New Jerseyan, Elias Boudinot. In his journal Boudinot gives a touching glimpse of Washington's kindness. The story also underscores the almost unbelievable degree to which his fellow Americans failed to support Washington in the war.

Boudinot at first refused the job, pointing out that the prisoners were starving, and the Americans had not a cent of money or supplies to send them. Washington's reply swiftly changed Boudinot's mind. "In much distress and with tears in his eyes he assured me that if he was deserted by the gentlemen of the country he should despair. He could not do everything. He was general, quartermaster, and commissary. Everything fell on him and he was unequal to the task. He gave me the most positive engagement that if I would contrive any mode for [the prisoners'] support and comfort, he would confirm it as far as was in his power—on this I told him that I knew of but one way and that was to borrow money on my own private security. He assured me that in case I did and was not reimbursed by Congress he would go an equal sharer with me in the loss.''

The British made many mistakes in fighting Washington. In none did they flounder more atrociously than in their attempts to humiliate him. King George's men began this game very early. In 1775, when Washington was besieging Boston, he received a letter from General William Howe, addressed to ''George Washington, Esquire.'' He promptly wrote a reply to ''William Howe, Esquire.''

The following year, as Howe was preparing to attack New York, another letter addressed to ''George Washington, Esquire, etc., etc.,'' was handed into the American lines. Washington ordered his aides to refuse it. A few days later the adjutant general of the British army asked for an interview with ''General Washington.'' Washington received him, wearing his full dress uniform. His epaulets plus his enormous height and frigidly correct manner had a shattering effect on the Britisher's composure. Stammering and spluttering, the adjutant tried to argue that George

Washington, Esquire & etc., & etc. was not intended to be disrespectful.

"Etc., etc. implies everything."

"So it does," growled Washington. "And anything."

General Howe soon gave up this little game. His successor, Henry Clinton, tried to revive it, whereupon Washington administered the *coup de grâce*. He took the letter, which was addressed to "Mr. Washington" and solemnly put it in his pocket. "This letter," he told the British officer who had delivered it, "is directed to a planter of the state of Virginia. I shall have it delivered to him after the end of the war. Till that time it shall not be opened." Within the hour Clinton's messenger was back with a duplicate addressed to "His Excellency General Washington."

Washington was not demanding personal obeisance. He was upholding the commissions of every man in his army and the right of the Continental Congress to grant them. There was another insult that Washington returned to the King's men with obvious personal relish. Not long after the debacle at Kips Bay, the British advance guard came within shooting distance of the retreating Americans. One of the British officers ordered his bugler to sound the "View, halloo," the call that means "fox in sight and on the run." It was, in its own way, a masterpiece of arrogance.

"I never felt such a sensation before," said one of Washington's aides. "It seemed to crown our disgrace."

Washington replied by throwing 1800 of his best men at the cocky British and driving them back over a mile. It was little more than a skirmish, though, and the American general obviously nursed in the back of his mind the wish to specifically revenge that fox call. It came on a frosty morning six months later, when he stormed out of the Princeton woods to send some of England's best regiments fleeing in headlong disorder. Pounding along beside his men, Washington whooped with delight at the sight of the running redcoats. "After them, my boys," he roared. "After them. It's a fine fox chase!"

8

Strength Versus Guile

WASHINGTON SELDOM MISSED AN OPPORTUNITY to needle the British for their emphasis on pompous ceremony. In the confused melee of the battle of Germantown, General Howe's dog lost track of his master and deserted to the Americans. With the elaborate formalities of a flag of truce, Washington returned the wandering canine to his opponent. An exact transcript of the letter with Washington's corrections of the draft written by an aide shows he still remembered being addressed as ''esquire'' by that unlucky general.

> General
> General Washington's compliments to ~~Sir~~ Wm. Howe. He does himself the pleasure to return his dog which accidentally fell into his hands and by the inscription on the collar appears to belong to ~~His Excellency~~ Sir William General Howe.

When misfortune befell an enemy general, Washington's instinctive generosity came to the fore. He interceded personally on behalf of ''Gentleman Johnny'' Burgoyne, captured at Saratoga, and persuaded Congress to permit him to go back to England on parole to defend himself against slanderous critics in Parliament. Washington wrote Burgoyne a letter, sympathizing ''with your feelings as a soldier.'' Burgoyne read it before the British Parliament, and declared that though it came from an enemy, ''it did credit to the human heart.''

Nevertheless, Washington never forgot he was fighting for his life. No general ever learned the art of total war faster than he did during the crisis-filled winter of 1776–77. What he could not win by strength he decided to win with guile—and forthwith became one of the most talented spy masters in history.

He had begun poorly in this department, too, sending amateur agent Nathan Hale to almost certain death by failing to maintain the slightest secrecy about his mission. As he retreated across the Delaware, Washington sent a rush messenger to Philadelphia for ''hard money'' to pay spies.

Within a matter of days he had recruited one of the cleverest agents of the war John Honeyman, an ex-British soldier who had kept his American patriotism a secret from his neighbors. Washington ordered Honeyman to desert to the protection of the Hessian garrison at Trenton. To cover his tracks Washington issued a stern proclamation denouncing him and offering rewards for his arrest. Loyal Americans were warned, however, to take the traitor alive because General Washington wanted the pleasure of hanging him personally.

In Trenton, meanwhile, Honeyman became the personal steward and warm friend of Colonel Johann Rall, the Hessian commander. After absorbing with a soldier's trained eye every last detail of Trenton's defenses, Honeyman had himself captured by an American patrol. Washington, putting on a performance worthy of an award, sternly denounced the "traitor" to his face and then ordered the room cleared, vowing he wanted to see if he could persuade this "dirty fellow" to support the American cause.

In a half hour Honeyman told Washington all he needed to know about Trenton. Washington threw open the door of his office and ordered the guard to clap Honeyman in jail and prepare for a hanging at dawn.

Toward evening a mysterious fire broke out near Washington's headquarters. The guards rushed to extinguish it. When they returned to the jailhouse, the door was open. Honeyman was gone!

Washington had, of course, supplied him with a key. For the benefit of the guards and his staff, the General exploded with rage, swore he would have them all court-martialed, and alerted the entire camp. Honeyman legged it past blazing muskets and by noon the following day was back in Trenton telling Colonel Rall all about his narrow escape. Rall naturally asked him if anything was stirring in the American camp. Honeyman regaled him with a vivid description of how the American army was close to total collapse from starvation and defeat.

Rall, already contemptuous of Americans, blithely proceeded with his Christmas celebrating. Honeyman quietly disappeared, and twelve hours later the Hessian colonel awoke to find Washington's ragged legions swarming on his doorstep.

In succeeding months, as his army dribbled away and Congress seemed incapable of finding new recruits (in March, 1777, he had 4,500 troops to the British 27,000), Washington pulled another sort of wool over British eyes. Going into winter quarters at Morristown, Washington distributed his men two and three to a house for miles along the main road. This gave everyone the impression that there was a huge force. A few days later, a refugee New York merchant trudged into camp, wailing grudges against the British. Washington instantly spotted him as a spy. Instead of arresting him, he ordered all his officers to treat the fellow with the greatest respect.

Secretly, Washington now ordered his brigadiers to prepare new, immensely exaggerated, figures on the army's current strength and send them to his headquarters. Washington then invited the bleating merchant to dinner and arranged to have himself called away at a crucial moment, carelessly leaving his papers unguarded on his desk. The spy's greedy eyes instantly devoured the fraudulent figures on the apparently official returns.

The next morning the spy vanished. In New York, the British commander, General William Howe, decided he could not dare attack 12,000 Americans entrenched in the rugged hills around Morristown, and once more Washington survived to fight another day.

A few weeks after this gambit, Washington began playing the double-agent game. He paid good money to a spy whom he knew was working for the British simply because the fellow was a convenient mouthpiece for sending in false information. He told one of his aides to keep a careful record of everything that was fabricated so that "if any other person should go in upon the same errand he may carry the same tale." Henceforth, Washington saw to it that the same fabrication reached the enemy by two, three, and even four different sources. A sample of his handiwork survives in a letter he sent a brigadier who was working with another double agent. "Copy it," Washington told him, "in an indifferent hand, preserving the bad spelling." The letter, a series of questions and answers, supposedly from a friend in the Continental camp, finished with a flourish, "When he left me he went strait to W's headquarters."

During the nearly disastrous winter at Valley Forge, Washington again bamboozled General Howe about the American army's strength and plans. This time he used an even bolder deception. He sent an agent to Howe with an offer to supply him with secret papers from "Washington's own files." Howe instantly swallowed the bait. For the next few months Washington industriously composed fraudulent returns on the army's strength, added memoranda about plans to attack Philadelphia and New York, and described other totally impossible stratagems. Because the "stolen" papers were in Washington's handwriting, Howe devoutly believed them. Washington and Major John Clark, the officer who supervised the comings and goings of the agents, seemed to have enjoyed themselves immensely as they wove this web of falsehood around their befuddled opponents. At one point, reporting on a particularly warm reception from Howe, Clark wrote to Washington, ''This will give you a laugh.''

By the time the war was three years old, Washington was operating as many as three separate spy networks inside the British lines in New York. (A key man in one of them was none other than James Rivington, publisher of *Rivington's Gazette*, a violently pro-British paper that was constantly lambasting the patriots.) Washington also developed his espionage technology. Sir James Jay, brother of New York patriot John Jay, developed a ''sympathetic'' writing fluid that remained totally invisible on white paper and could be made visible only by brushing it with another chemical solution. All of Washington's spies were using this device by late 1779. They usually wrote the secret message at the bottom of sensible business letters, always addressed to known Tories to make the bearer look extra loyal.

These New York spies played a vital role in avoiding a potential disaster. In 1779, Sir Henry

By 1779, Washington's strategy of patience and surprise had earned him a reputation as a brilliant military leader.

Clinton planned to attack the French troops who had just landed in Newport, Rhode Island. Working with frantic haste, one of Washington's networks got word to his headquarters in New Jersey written with the invisible ink. Washington instantly arranged to have "secret" papers captured by loyalist irregulars. The papers contained elaborate plans for an attack on New York, and the British hastily abandoned their expedition to Newport.

Washington never let a spy down. Once, Tory raiders captured the secret papers and codes of one of Washington's espionage colonels. Washington instantly wrote, ''The person most endangered by the loss of your papers is one Higday . . . who lives not far from the Bowery on the island of New York. I wish you would endeavor to give him the speediest notice of what has happened.'' An agent slipped into New York, warned Higday, and Higday had a cover story ready when the British arrested him. He survived to spy some more.

No wonder the British called Washington ''the old fox.''

Another, equally unknown Washington is the shrewd controversialist who fought and defeated a vicious, well-organized conspiracy to deprive him of his command. It began, ironically, in the fall of 1777 with an act of generosity on Washington's part. Although he was battling the British for the American capital, Philadelphia, he dispatched 3,000 of his best troops, including Daniel Morgan's Virginia riflemen, to assist Major General Horatio Gates, who was confronting another British army at Saratoga.

Washington lost his battles to save Philadelphia. Gates won at Saratoga. Almost from the
moment of victory, Gates began scheming for
Washington's job. Backing him was the group of
disgruntled New Englanders in Congress who
had regretted choosing Washington from the
start. John Adams, while not one of these petty
schemers, was typical of those who were alarmed
by the adulation heaped on Washington by some
of his admirers. After Saratoga, he wrote his wife,
''Now we can allow a certain citizen to be wise,
virtuous and good, without thinking him a deity
or a savior.''

Gates did not even bother to send Washington,
his commander-in-chief, news of the victory.
Washington learned about it only when one of his
aides stopped a dispatch rider carrying the news
to Congress and borrowed the letter to show the
General. Washington's first reaction was typical
of the man he had become. There were already
rumors among his aides that Gates was intriguing
against him. Yet when he saw that the British had
surrendered at Saratoga, he passed the letter to
one of his aides, signifying that he wished him to
read it aloud. As the aide finished it, all eyes
turned to Washington. Colonel Timothy Pickering, who often told the story, always recalled his
amazement to discover on Washington's face

nothing but the most unfeigned joy. Although Pickering declined to call Washington a great general, he never from that moment denied he was a great man. He used to say that for him Washington represented ''humanity in its noblest grandeur—a man to whom self was nothing, his country everything.''

Washington was far too realistic not to see Gates and his friends were out to destroy him. Again, we see remarkable evidence of Washington's growth. Instead of lashing out at his tormentors, he said and did exactly nothing and let them make the first mistake.

Congress rammed through an insulting resolution forbidding Washington to withdraw more than 2500 men from Gates's army. Another patriot, Benjamin Rush, who flattered Washington to his face, sent out a flood of anonymous critical letters calling for Washington's replacement. Gates himself began slyly approaching other generals, murmuring about the dissatisfaction with Washington in the main army and the danger to the cause. Soon the web of conspirators included Thomas Conway, a French-trained Irishman who had won a brigadier general's commission from Congress. A born flatterer, he wrote Gates a series of letters criticizing the American army, including such apostrophes as "what a pity there is but one Gates."

For all their clacking, the conspirators did not accomplish much. One of Rush's unsigned hate letters was forwarded to Washington by Patrick Henry, now governor of Virginia. "I am sorry," Henry wrote, "there should be one man who counts himself my friend who is not yours." When Gates murmured his hints about replacing Washington to Colonel Daniel Morgan, he got for an answer, "I have one favor to ask of you which is never to mention that detestable subject to me again; for under no other man than Washington will I ever serve."

Gates's supporters soon realized they did not have enough strength in Congress to oust Washington. They contented themselves with making Gates president of the "Board of War," a quasi-legislative body that was supposed to coordinate the war effort on a continental scale. Gates, meanwhile, used Conway's critical letters as a screen, circulating them freely among his cronies in the hope that they spoke for themselves. Still Washington did nothing.

Then came the indiscretion he was waiting for. One of Gates's aides, James Wilkinson, had dinner with General Lord Stirling, who was totally loyal to Washington. Wilkinson got drunk and proceeded to repeat several passages from Conway's letters. Stirling promptly forwarded them to Washington.

Washington sat down and wrote a two-sentence letter to General Conway.

Sir: A letter which I received last night contained the following paragraph.

"In a letter from General Conway to General Gates he says heaven has been determined to save your country or a weak general and bad counselors would have ruined it."

I am, sir, your humble servant,

George Washington

This simple query hit the conspirators with the impact of heavy cannon shot. Conway rushed to Washington and denied writing those particular words. Gates, hearing from others that Washington was on his trail, became completely rattled and shot the ground out from under Conway by writing a blustery letter admitting the whole correspondence but accusing Washington of hiring a spy to copy off his private mail.

Washington, playing his hand like a professional card shark, wrote acidly to Gates. "I never knew that General Conway, who I viewed in the light of a stranger to you, was a correspondent of yours, much less did I suspect that I was the subject of your confidential letters." He went on to say that his original impression, since Gates's aide had supplied the information, was that Gates was sending him a friendly warning against a "secret enemy."

Then with whiplash sarcasm, he added, "But in this, as in other matters of late, I have found myself mistaken."

Washington sent a copy of his letter to Congress and sat back to watch the conspiracy collapse into something very close to farce. Everyone involved began accusing everyone else of lying. Gates denounced Wilkinson to the Board of War and was challenged to a duel by his garrulous former aide. When they met on the street, Gates broke down and wept and Wilkinson accepted his apology. Conway went home to France.

For two more years Gates continued to snipe at Washington from his theoretically lofty position on the Board of War. Then he rode south to rescue the Carolinas from a rampaging British army led by Lord Cornwallis. Relying largely on militia, Gates challenged Cornwallis at Camden, North Carolina, and within an hour lost both his army and his reputation. Riding the fastest horse he could find, he did not stop retreating until he was 160 miles behind the lines. There were hoots of laughter and demands for a court-martial from many Americans, but Washington never said a word that could be used against his fallen adversary. It took two years for a dawdling Congress to clear Gates of any blame. Immediately, Washington offered Gates command of the right wing of the American army. He accepted and served loyally until the end of the war.

When we realize that Washington was grappling with this conspiracy while simultaneously trying to preserve the remnants of an army in the freezing hell of Valley Forge, his self-control is even more remarkable. It was during these same discouraging months that Washington performed an extraordinary act of generosity for his old friend Bryan Fairfax. By now Bryan had become an acknowledged Loyalist. At a time when the British were tempting patriots such as Elias Boudinot with 10,000 pounds and a dukedom, Washington risked a great deal to see Bryan at all. The Gates men could have used it as a canard to question his loyalty. Yet Washington received Bryan with all the friendship and hospitality he invariably showed him during the years of peace at Mount Vernon and gave him a safe-conduct pass through the Continental lines to British-held New York. There Fairfax was so discouraged by the attitude and demands of His Majesty's officials, he returned to Virginia and wrote a letter that was perhaps the finest tribute anyone paid Washington's genius for friendship.

> That at a time when your popularity was at the highest and mine at the lowest, and when it is so common for men's resentments to run high against those who differ from them in opinion, you should act with your wanted kindness towards me has affected me more than any favor I have received; and could not be believed by some in New York, it being above the run of common minds.

9

Wisdom and Victory

WASHINGTON THE SELF-SATISFIED young provincial who equated ignorance with speaking a foreign language also vanished in the crucible of war. Germans such as Friedrich Steuben, Poles such as Tadeusz Kosciuszko, his old enemies the French—Washington took them all into his army and won not only their respect but their affection. He was equally indifferent to religious prejudice. Catholics were harassed by prohibitory laws in most colonies. Colonel Stephen Moylan, one of Washington's favorite staff officers, was the brother of the Archbishop of Cork. Several times after the French became America's allies Washington attended Catholic Mass with them, a gesture which Benedict Arnold, of all people, tried to use against him after he defected to the British.

Once, at Valley Forge, Washington's broad-minded approach prevented a serious mutiny. On

St. Patrick's Day, some New England and Pennsylvania troops began parading a "stuffed Paddy"—a highly uncomplimentary image of St. Patrick—around the camp.

In a fury, the numerous Irish in the American ranks reached for their guns and marched on their tormentors. Their officers lost control of them and called for help from Washington.

He quickly rode to the scene and patiently listened to the angry Gaels' complaints. "Point out the offenders to me," Washington said, "and I will see that they are punished."

This left the Irish on one foot. They answered lamely that they had no specific accusations to make.

"Well," said Washington, "I too am a lover of St. Patrick's Day and must settle the affair by making all the army keep the day."

He forthwith ordered an extra ration of rum for every man in the camp and in the words of an aide, "all made merry and were good friends."

Bryan Fairfax was by no means Washington's only link with his Virginia life. Throughout the war years, Martha Washington traveled north every winter to share the hardships and dangers of camp life. The timid worrisome Martha whom Washington had feared to leave alone became another woman in these years of crisis, braving a

700-mile round trip over swollen rivers and along impassable roads to be at her husband's side. She was badly needed. In the winter of 1777, she arrived in time to nurse Washington back to health from a bout of influenza. A few weeks before she arrived he was so sick he feared he was on his deathbed and appointed Nathanael Greene as his successor.

Disease and bad roads were not the only hazards Martha had to face. In camp, Washington was surrounded by a group of picked troops, known as his "Life Guards." These men were sworn to defend the person of the commander-in-chief with their lives if necessary. One of the constant American fears was an attempt to kidnap Washington. Britian's vast superiority in cavalry had enabled them to swoop down and seize Major General Charles Lee in 1776. Every time there was an alarm from a sentry, the Life Guards were under orders to charge from their tents and station five armed men at every window of Washington's house, turning it into a small fortress. Many nights Martha had to shiver under the covers while these burly fighters tumbled into her room and poised their loaded muskets at her window.

Winter camp life was not all danger and hardship. Other officers followed Washington's example and brought their wives to camp too. The ladies awoke the dancer in Washington, and he was soon organizing a series of balls. Martha had grown plump and apparently preferred the spectator's role at these affairs. Other ladies were more than willing to replace her, notably Katherine Greene, the lively and beautiful wife of Washington's second in command.

One evening, Katherine Greene enthusiastically announced she could dance forever. Washington gallantly challenged her to prove it. They advanced to the floor and proceeded to stay there for three consecutive hours when Mrs. Greene, who was only half Washington's age, laughingly surrendered.

Such lighthearted exploits should go far toward making us realize Washington was anything but a man on a pedestal to those who knew him well. Another amusement of camp days was playing ''base'' or wicket with his junior aides. This was a forerunner of baseball, played with a large, soft ball and a flat bat. Washington reportedly took great satisfaction in proving he could throw as hard and sprint as fast as his young assistants. At other times, when there was no chance to organize a game, he was fond of just throwing a ball back and forth in front of headquarters.

Washington did not have a fund of funny stories, as Lincoln did, but he firmly believed, as he wrote a friend, "It was better to go laughing than crying through life." At Valley Forge he ordered that every time an officer or private got drunk he must dig out one of the innumerable tree stumps that the men left behind from their hut building. In a matter of weeks there was only one stump left. A few days later, as he rode past, Washington found this remnant being hacked from the ground by an unhappy celebrator.

"Well, my good fellow, you have found the last stump," Washington said.

"Yes," the man growled, "and now when an officer gets drunk there'll be no stump to cut."

Washington laughed heartily and rode on.

He was not above having a laugh at the expense of his favorite officers when the occasion called for it. One day, during the siege of Boston, headquarters was alarmed by a warning of a British attack. Everyone leaped up and dashed for swords and coats. Nathanael Greene scampered about, furiously demanding his wig, which was on the top of his head all the time. Someone finally said to him, "Your wig is behind the looking glass, sir." When Greene looked in the mirror, Washington collapsed on the nearest sofa in uproarious laughter.

He could also be something of a tease. When one of his horses threw his aide, William Jackson, Washington promptly named the horse "Jackson." One suspects Washington had a hand in naming a headquarters cat "Hamilton" (though it was blamed on Martha) because it was a Tom and very popular with the females in the neighborhood, a talent of which aide Alexander Hamilton frequently boasted. After the war, Washington was entertaining his ex-aide Colonel David Humphreys at Mount Vernon. Washington was extremely fond of Humphreys. He was a distinguished poet and man of letters, everything that Washington was not, and it must have been a little tiring, at times, to put up with his frequent quotations from literature and his general air of high culture. One day, while they were out riding, Humphreys began disputing his chief on a subject he should have avoided: horsemanship. Soon he was challenging Washington to leap a nearby hedge.

"You go first," Washington said.

Humphreys sailed gallantly over the barrier to land with a huge splash in a mud hole on the other side. Washington cantered up to the safe side of the hedge and peered over at Humphreys, up to his saddle in swamp water, and said, "Ah, Colonel, you are too deep for me."

There were other times when Washington's sarcasm could approach wit. Toward the end of the war, someone remarked that the American Superintendent of Finance had his hands full. ''I wish he had his pockets full,'' said Washington. Inviting two of his officers and their wives to dinner at West Point, he demolished his cook as follows:

> Since our arrival at this happy spot, we have had a ham . . . to grace the head of the table; a piece of roast beef adorns the foot; and a dish of beans, (almost imperceptible) decorates the center. When the cook has a mind to cut a figure (which I presume will be the case tomorrow) we have two beef steak pyes, or dishes of crabs in addition, one on each side of the center dish, dividing the space and reducing the distance between dish and dish to about six feet, which without them would be near 12 feet apart. Of late he has had the surprising sagacity to discover that apples will make pyes; and it's a question if, in the violence of his efforts, we do not get one of apples, instead of having both of beef steaks. If the ladies can put up with such entertainment . . . I shall be happy to see them.

Though Washington was usually a gallant gentleman with the ladies, there were times when his days as an unlucky courter of Virginia belles stood him in good stead. A young officer once came to him and begged for leave to see his sweetheart, who was supposedly pining away for lack of his company. With an experienced smile, Washington turned him down. "Women don't die of such things," he said.

At still other times he could sound like a very well-wedded man. To the Marquis de Chastellux, on learning of his marriage he wrote wryly, "So your day has at last come . . . Now you are well served for coming to fight in favor of the American rebels, all the way across the Atlantic ocean, by catching that terrible contagion, domestic felicity, which like the smallpox or the plague, a man can have only once in his life . . ."

Sometimes the measure of a man can be glimpsed in little things. One of Washington's most consistent traits was his consideration for other people, their comfort, their health, even their feelings. A visitor to Mount Vernon told of waking in the middle of the night with a very dry throat that soon became a racking cough. Suddenly a hand parted the curtains beside his bed, and there stood the master of Mount Vernon, himself, with a cup of hot tea for his guest.

When Washington left the house he had made his winter quarters in Morristown, he ordered an exact inventory of every item in the building to be sure nothing was missing. The account was presented to the owner who reported only a single tiny loss: a tablespoon. A few months later there arrived in the mail from Mount Vernon a single spoon with the initials "G.W." on it.

In his presidential years during a tour of the South, Washington, traveling along intolerably dusty roads, sent one of his servants ahead with a formal letter announcing his arrival at the house where he hoped to spend the night. Scrawled on the bottom beneath the dignified official document was a P.S. from the President: "For God's sake give my man some grog!"

There were also times when Washington could be hard and cold. When a raiding party of American Loyalists captured and hanged an American militia captain, Washington demanded that their leader be hanged in return. The British demurred. Washington grimly selected by lot a young captain among the British prisoners of war and announced he would hang him to balance off the murdered American. Only the intercession of King Louis XVI of France, to whom the mother of the captain sent a plea, changed Washington's mind. Meanwhile, Tory raiders were very careful with their prisoners.

One other time Washington had to summon all the resolution in him to order an unwanted and distasteful death: the execution of Major John André. This gallant and attractive young man had been captured while conspiring with the traitor Benedict Arnold to seize the vital American fortress at West Point on the Hudson. The British argued that he had landed under a flag of truce and he was, therefore, not a spy. Washington replied, "Major André was employed in the execution of measures very foreign to the object of flags of truce and such as they were never meant to authorize or countenance in the most distant degree; and this gentleman confessed with the greatest candor in the course of his examination that it was impossible for him to suppose that he came ashore under the sanction of the flag."

André's personality charmed all the Americans he met. Many came to Washington and pleaded for him. Washington was inflexible. He offered only one concession: he would exchange André for Arnold. The British refused. When a court-martial found André guilty and condemned him to death, Washington, with a hand that reportedly shook, wrote the fateful words: "The Commander-in-Chief directs the execution of the above sentence in the usual way this afternoon at 5 o'clock precisely."

André died like the brave man he was and the British condemned Washington as a murderer. It was a grim, even an impossible, decision Washington had to make. To have shown compassion at a moment when the American war effort was sinking to its lowest ebb, when many were talking of a compromise peace, could easily have become the first sign of weakness, surrender.

Washington was a leader. A leader must make such hard, heartbreaking decisions. Those who follow, who serve in the ranks, forget the loneliness of those at the helm, but there are times when they are all too grateful for their presence. A year after André's death, Washington and a group of French officers visited West Point and decided to return by boat to headquarters at New Windsor, some five miles upstream. It was winter, and the river was full of rushing, cracking ice. The wind began to blow hard, and the Hudson's formidable waves crashed over the bow. As they neared their rocky landing place, there was a veritable surf running. The master of the oarsmen lost his nerve and swore the wallowing boat was going down. Panic swept the passengers until Washington put out his big hand. "Courage, my friends," he called. "I will steer. My place is at the helm." With skill undoubtedly derived from many hours on his native Potomac, he landed them safely.

This fatherly spirit grew steadily in Washington as the war progressed. In his youth, he had been helped by older men. As commander-in-chief, he returned the generosity tenfold. He was constantly on the lookout for talented young men to serve as his aides. He became extremely fond of most of them and followed (and often pushed) their careers for the rest of his life.

Washington chose these men with care, generally requiring two not-always compatible qualifications: brains and courage. Twenty-year-old Alexander Hamilton first recommended himself for the fierceness with which he fought his company of New York artillery in the assaults on Trenton and Princeton. Hamilton, however, was the exception among these young men whom Washington, in the style of the time, called his "family." Though Washington showed him every sign of favor and effection, he was never able to win more than grudging admiration from this ambitious, coldly brilliant young West Indian. A perceptive man like Washington undoubtedly sensed this reserve; and it explains in part the angry scene with which Hamilton ended his service as an aide.

According to Hamilton, he passed Washington on the stairs at headquarters. Washington told Hamilton he wanted to speak to him; Hamilton answered that he would come the moment he had delivered an important letter, which he had in his hand, to the commissary. On his way back

Hamilton found himself accosted by the Marquis de Lafayette and they talked "about a minute on a matter of business." When Hamilton reached the top of the stairs, he found Washington waiting for him.

"Colonel Hamilton," he said, "you have kept me waiting at the head of these stairs these ten minutes. I must tell you, sir, you treat me with disrespect."

"I am not conscious of it, sir," Hamilton replied, "but since you have thought it necessary to tell me so, we part."

Within the hour Washington sent another aide, Tench Tilghman, to Hamilton to apologize. Incredibly, Hamilton refused, informing Tilghman that he had "taken my resolution in a manner not to be revoked."

Hamilton then demanded absolute secrecy from Washington about the clash—and proceeded to write his version of it to several friends. Nevertheless, when Hamilton demanded charge of a Continental regiment, Washington, with that astounding ability to ignore petty failings and see the essential man and his value to the cause, went to great trouble to find him a command. A few months later, at the climactic assault on Yorktown, Washington gave his contentious ex-favorite leadership of a crucial storming party—an honor coveted by every officer in the army. Hamilton justified Washington's judgment by fighting magnificently.

With another young man Washington was more successful in winning not merely admiration, but love. At first glance, nothing would seem more unlikely or incongruous than a friendship between this reticent Virginian in his late forties and the Marquis de Lafayette, a twenty-one-year-old scion of powdered and privileged French nobility. Within six months of their meeting, Lafayette was calling Washington his ''adopted father.'' (His own had been killed in battle when he was an infant.) Perhaps he awoke in Washington a yearning for the son Martha never bore him. There are other explanations. Washington detested anyone who lied or faked. Lafayette was sincerity itself, incapable of holding back what he thought and felt. His loyalty to Washington was absolute. In the beginning of the intrigue against Washington, Conway and several other officers invited Lafayette to dinner and tried to lure the Marquis from his allegiance. His answer was a toast to Washington's health which the chagrined conspirators were forced to drink.

Once stirred, Washington's affection was intense. Some months after Lafayette returned to France to secure additional French aid, Washington had dinner with a French friend and eagerly inquired after him. The man gave a glowing picture of Lafayette's popularity for his achievements in America. ''Washington blushed like a fond father whose child is being praised,'' the Frenchman wrote. ''Tears fell from his eyes. He clasped my hand and could hardly utter the words, 'I do not know a finer soul and I love him as my own son.' ''

Perhaps the most astonishing evidence of how far emotion could carry Washington was his reunion with Lafayette outside Williamsburg a few weeks before Yorktown. To the amazement of the watching Americans, Lafayette hurled himself at Washington, clasped him in his arms, and kissed him ''from ear to ear once or twice with as much ardor as ever an absent lover kissed his mistress on return,'' according to one observer.

Fond as he was of Lafayette, however, Washington never let emotions interfere with his judgment. In 1778, when Lafayette concocted a grandiose scheme to lead an expedition to conquer Canada, arguing that he alone could win the sympathy of the French enclave there, Washington vetoed the plan as utterly impossible for an army so close to disintegration. Lafayette bombarded Congress with complaints that the cancellation would reflect on his reputation in Europe. When

Congress wrote sympathetically to Washington about the Marquis's hurt feelings, his adopted father replied somewhat curtly that his ''fears are excited only by an uncommon degree of sensibility.''

In another letter Washington even expressed a suspicion that Lafayette might not have originated the scheme but was actually the tool of the French cabinet. With clear-eyed realism that foreshadowed the statesmanship of his Presidency, Washington pointed out that if France reconquered Canada, they would, thanks to their possession of New Orleans and their influence with the Indians on the frontier, completely surround the American states. This, he feared, would be ''too great a temptation to be resisted by any power.'' Much as he wanted to think the best thoughts of America's new ally, he believed it ''a maxim founded on the universal experience of mankind that no nation is to be trusted farther than it is bound by its interests.''

It was this tough, shrewd realism that enabled Washington to win the Revolutionary War. When he saw that he would never be able to muster from the disorganized colonies an army powerful enough to expel the British, he accepted the premise of a long war and fought that way, husbanding his scarecrow regiments, striking only when the

British gave him an opening. Numerous wit-
nesses testify to how he carried the Revolution on
his broad shoulders. Chevalier de Fleury, a hard-
fighting French volunteer, wrote this assessment
of the war in 1779. ''Congress is divided . . . in
spite of the names of France and England, country and liberty with which they hide their mutual
animosities, the secret motive of their intrigues,
their cabals, their everlasting barking, is individual hatred or that between state and state . . .
General Washington is the Atlas of America.''

Other men gave up and abandoned Congress
and the army. Some went eagerly, to play politics
in their native states, some reluctantly, torn between a wish to serve and a desperate need to
recoup personal finances, ruined by the collapse
of Continental currency. Others simply buckled
under the spiritual and physical strain. Washington stayed. Day after day, week after week,
month after month, year after dragging year, he
struggled with the endless shortages of food and
money, court martials, and resignations. Tire-
lessly the letters, reports, memorandums, orders
of the day flowed out. To get some idea of the
fantastic amount of work this man produced, stop
in a public library some day and ask to see the
collected writings of Washington. They fill shelf
after shelf, thirty-nine volumes, more than 25,000
separate documents, and well over half were writ-

ten during the eight exhausting years of the Revolution.

There were times when even he yielded to despair, when he wrote lamentations in letters or in his diary that are worthy of a Jeremiah. Often he seemed more Job than Atlas. For the first six months of 1781 everything seemed to go wrong. Whole brigades mutinied. The British intercepted a personal letter Washington wrote to his cousin in Virginia, criticizing French efforts to relieve that embattled state. Only his honesty rescued him from a diplomatic gaffe of the first rank. He frankly admitted he had written the letter and the French commander, Comte de Rochambeau, could do only the gracious thing and forget it.

Then there was even more dismaying news from Virginia. British raiders had been burning houses up and down the Potomac. When an enemy ship stopped near Mount Vernon, Lund Washington, the plantation manager, had obsequiously gone on board, given the King's men food, and humbly asked them to return Mount Vernon's runaway slaves. Mournfully Washington wrote Lund, ''It would have been less painful to have heard . . . that they had burnt my house and laid the plantation in ruins. You ought to have considered yourself as my representative and should have reflected on the bad example . . .''

Then he learned that his mother had been

pleading poverty so loudly that the Virginia Assembly was considering a motion to grant her a
pension. Rarely was Washington so mortified. He
wrote a long letter declaring that Mrs. Washington did not have a child who "would not di-
vide the last sixpence to relieve her from *real* distress."

Still Washington hung on through the do-
nothing summer of 1781 until fall, when Yorktown gave him the winning card he had been
waiting to pull from destiny's deck. It was, in
essence, the same combination that had won him
all his victories: a blizzard of rumors and false
intelligence, a secret march, a sudden attack
where the enemy least expected it.

While the allied army lingered outside New
York, double agents deluged the British with fake
American plans for an attack on this citadel of
British power. Washington himself spent an hour
one day asking a known Tory sympathizer questions about landing beaches and routes of march
on Long Island. Then he sternly cautioned the
fellow not to mention a word about his interest to
anyone. "I have no doubt," said an admiring
American who watched the performance, "that
the British general heard about it that night."

Vast ovens were constructed in New Jersey,
implying preparations for a permanent siege

camp. When the French and Americans proceeded to march away across New Jersey on the
first leg of their journey south to trap Cornwallis
at Yorktown, the British remained convinced until
the allies were well south of Philadelphia that the
whole maneuver was a feint to disguise an attack
on New York via Staten Island.

Only once on the march to Yorktown did
Washington show a sign of what the victory
meant to him emotionally. When he heard that
Admiral De Grasse had arrived in the Ches-
apeake, bottling Cornwallis in the indefensible
little tobacco port, he hastened to tell the news to
his brother general, Rochambeau. He met the
commander of the French Expeditionary Force at
Chester, Pennsylvania. Thus far the relations between the two men had been friendly, but very
proper. Now while Rochambeau's vessel approached the wharf (he made part of the journey
by ship), Washington pulled out his handkerchief
and took off his hat and swung them both in
great exultant circles. When Rochambeau stepped
off the ship, Washington flung his arms about
him and whooped the good news.

"I have never seen a man moved by a greater
or more sincere joy than was General Washington," stated one of Rochambeau's officers.
Another said he seemed to "put aside his charac-

ter as arbiter of North America and contented himself for the moment with that of a citizen happy at the good fortune of his country.''

On a dark and rainy night the engineering troops moved out to dig Yorktown's siege trenches. Only 200 yards from British lines, the jittery men were interrupted by a tall man in a black cloak. They first thought he was a civilian, possibly a spy, and considered braining him with their picks and shovels. Only when he spoke did they realize, with a gasp, that it was Washington, sharing the worst risks with his men.

A few days later, reconnoitering the British lines, a cannonball came so close to Washington and his party that it showered them with flying dirt. Washington did not even turn his head; he continued to study the British fortifications through his field glass. A shaken chaplain, who happened to be in the group, took off his hat to show Washington how much dirt he had collected in the crown. ''Mr. Evans,'' Washington replied with a smile, ''you had better carry that home and show it to your wife and children.''

When Yorktown reached its thunderously successful conclusion, Washington sent the news to Congress in the simplest, most unadorned victory dispatch any victorious general ever sent an anxious senate. The message began: ''Sir, I have the

On October 19, 1781, British forces surrendered to General Washington at Yorktown, Virginia.

Honor to inform Congress that a Reduction of the British Army under the Command of Lord Cornwallis, is most happily effected.'' Then, without the smallest reference to himself, he proceeded to give the credit to his men: ''The unremitting ardor which actuated every officer and soldier in the combined army on this occasion has principally led to this important event at an earlier period than my most sanguine hope had induced me to expect . . .''

Only the soldier in Washington gave the surrender a small touch of drama. With Rochambeau beside him, he rode out to the captured British redoubts within a stone's throw of their main lines and waited there for Cornwallis to send out the signed document of capitulation. When it came, Washington signed it in the saddle and added: ''Done in the trenches before Yorktown. October 19, 1781.''

That same afternoon, when the British marched out to lay down their arms, they tried one last gambit in their six-year war of protocol. Cornwallis pleaded sickness and did not appear at the head of his troops. Instead he sent his second in command. Washington was ready for them once more. He smoothly stepped aside and allowed the British to surrender to *his* second in command.

The moment the surrender was over, he was magnanimity itself to his prisoners. At a dinner for Cornwallis and his officers, Rochambeau offered a toast to the King of France. Cornwallis lamely offered a response simply to ''the King.'' Washington, holding up his glass, added what Cornwallis was thinking. ''Of England,'' he said. ''Confine him there and I'll drink him a full bumper.''

10

The Secret Crisis

YORKTOWN BROUGHT WASHINGTON HOME to Virginia after six years of war. Home to the places and faces he loved most. Home to victory and, alas, to tragedy. Jack Custis had for once overcome his mother's fears and joined the army as a temporary aide on Washington's staff. He fell victim of the dysentery which was so common in all armies at that time. Washington sent him to nearby Eltham, home of his aunt, ordered Dr. Craik to care for him, and summoned Martha, Jack's wife, Nellie, and his children, from Mount Vernon. The best available medical skill and tenderest care were useless. Three weeks after Yorktown, Washington rode all night to reach Eltham at dawn to find Jack dying. Disappointing as Jack had been in many ways, he had a wonderful charm and Washington loved him deeply. When Dr. Craik told him there was no hope he is said to have flung himself on a bed in grief. In a few moments he composed himself and went to comfort the two weeping women.

A week later he paid a ceremonial visit to his mother. It must have been for Washington another deeply emotional moment. There he stood at forty-nine, the son she had tried so hard to tame at her apron strings, conqueror of the world's mightiest empire. According to the family tradition, his mother did not say a single complimentary word to him. She called him George, worried about his health, noting how tired he looked after six years of war, then reminisced about old times and old friends. "But of his glory, not one word."

Nevertheless, she did consent to attend a dance at Fredericksburg in his honor, entering the room on her son's arm, accepting with him the storm of applause. She stayed only a few minutes, then announced "it is high time for old folks to be in bed," and had George escort her home. Washington came back to the party and soon convinced his old friends and neighbors that the British had not worn him down. In the shank of the evening, according to one eye witness, he "went down some dozen couple in the contre dance with great spirit and satisfaction."

For Washington, Yorktown was by no means

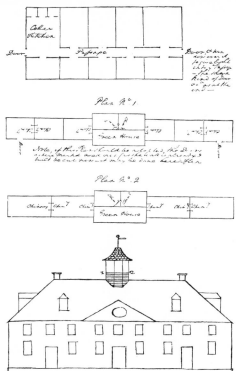

The Washington estate at Mount Vernon was built in 1743 by George's half-brother, Lawrence. George undertook major renovations beginning in 1773, adding the wings and portico.

the end of the war. He was able to linger only two days at his beloved Mount Vernon, and then he rode north again for two more years of coping with a lackadaisical Congress and the reluctant states. Although there was no fighting, he saw it was absolutely necessary to keep an army together so that American diplomats could negotiate from strength at the peace table. It was the same old story, with food and clothing in short supply and money nonexistent. As rumors of imminent peace became more insistent, ominous signs of revolt appeared in the discontented army.

The trouble began with a sober memorandum submitted to Washington at headquarters by one of his colonels, arguing that the only hope of governing the country sensibly lay in a monarchy with George Washington as king. ''Be assured, sir,'' Washington wrote in reply, ''no occurrence in the course of the war has given me more painful sensations than your information of there being such ideas existing in the army . . . Let me conjure you if you have any regard for your country, concern for yourself or posterity or respect for me, to banish those thoughts from your mind . . .''

Then Congress, bungling as usual, decided to welsh on promises it had made to the officers in regard to their back pay and a bonus of five years' pay or half pay for life. Already reduced to selling their uniforms for vegetables and using their ammunition to kill game, the desperate men exploded. A handbill was circulated, a rabble-rousing call to arms if there ever was one. "Can you consent to be the only sufferers by this Revolution?" it shrieked. A few days later, another, even more inflamatory, message was distributed. "If peace takes place, never unsheath your swords until you have obtained full and ample justice."

Two days later, Washington called a meeting of the officers in a big log building called "the Temple," with a raised platform at one end. This moment, so little known by those who love to paint the Revolution in glowing terms, was the real crisis in the nation's birth. America stood at a crossroads on March 12th, 1783, as these tough, angry men filed into that crude building and Washington and his general officers walked out on the stage. It was entirely in the power of George Washington to send America down that bloody, bitter path that almost every other revolution in the history of the world has followed: a dictatorship built on the army's bayonets. Oliver Cromwell had done it in England. Napoleon would do it in France, Lenin in Russia, and every nation in South America would commit the same terrible blunder. The American army was ready, even willing, to do it on that harrowing day in 1783, until George Washington rose to address them.

He walked to a lectern at the front of the stage and addressed "his brother officers." He called upon them to renounce the proposals of the anonymous handbills and vowed he would do everything in his power to win justice from Congress. He implored them not to take any measures which "viewed in the calm light of reason will lessen the dignity and sully the glory you have hitherto maintained." He urged them instead to "afford occasion for posterity to say when speaking of the glorious example you have exhibited to mankind, had this day been wanting, the world had never seen the last stage of perfection to which human nature is capable of attaining."

Then Washington began reading a letter from Joseph Jones, a congressman from Virginia who was sympathetic to the claims of the army. His eyes, worn from so many hours of reading and writing dispatches by candlelight, could not make out the closely written sentences. He reached into his pocket and took out new spectacles, which he had recently received from Philadelphia. "Gentlemen," he said as he fumbled with the glasses, "you must pardon me. I have grown gray in your service and now find myself growing blind."

The simplicity and truth of this statement struck every heart in the hall. Dozens of these hard-bitten veterans wept openly. Washington finished the letter and left the stage. A few moments later the men voted to repudiate the mutinous handbills and place their hopes for the future in Washington's hands.

Back in his headquarters, Washington demanded justice for his men in a letter that scorched the ears of Congress. "If retiring from the field they are to grow old in poverty, wretchedness, and contempt, if they are to wade through the vile mire of dependency and owe the miserable remnant of that life to charity which has hitherto been spent in honor, then shall I have learned what ingratitude is. Then shall I have realized a tale which will embitter every moment of my future life."

Within the month, news of peace arrived and Congress voted to pay the departing officers full pay for five years. The Revolution had been rescued.

This was the negative side of Washington's final achievement as a Revolutionary leader. He had saved the Revolution from plunging down the path of self-destruction. Now he turned his mind to guiding it along the path to national achievement. His farewell letter as commander-in-chief of the army was sent to the governors and legislatures of the thirteen states. In it, with keen foresight, he criticized the ramshackle Articles of Confederation by which the nation was attempting to govern itself and called for "an indissoluble union of the states under one federal head." He also called on the people of the United States "to forget their local prejudices and policies, to make those mutual concessions which are requisite to the general prosperity and in some instances to sacrifice their individual advantages to the interest of the community." But the "indissoluble union" was his main point. "Whatever measures have a tendency to dissolve the union or contribute to violate or lessen a sovereign authority ought to be considered as hostile to the liberty and independency of America and the authors of them treated accordingly."

It took four years for Washington's fellow citizens to realize the wisdom of these words. Only then did a Constitutional Convention finally meet in Philadelphia and hammer out a plan by which the quarrelsome, contentious states became a united America. The man who presided over this group of brilliant architects as president of the Convention was George Washington. When the battle over ratification of the Constitution divided the country, it was George Washington, again, who did more than any other man to win the nation's approval. In Virginia's ratifying convention, without making a single speech, he carried the day against fulminating Patrick Henry and a chorus of other orators, winning by a mere five votes. For most Americans, it was enough to know that George Washington approved the Constitution.

They also voted yea with the assurance that George Washington would be the man to administer that Constitution as first president. Letters poured into Mount Vernon from men of influence in all parts of the nation, urging the task upon him. Washington recoiled at first. He said the idea cast "a kind of gloom upon my mind." He was fifty-seven years old and had, through eight years of toil and trouble, earned enough honor and reputation to satisfy any man. Now he was being asked to risk his good name again on a battlefield he feared and disliked, the gray and tricky landscape of politics. It meant another farewell to his beloved Mount Vernon and the inevitable neglect of this and his many other farmlands. (Only in the few years of Washington's personal supervision did Mount Vernon show a profit.) But when the electoral college voted unanimously to make him the first president, he accepted the task as another call from his country in crisis.

"I go to the chair of government," he wrote his old friend Henry Knox, "with feelings not unlike those of a culprit who is going to the place of his execution." But he also went with an iron determination to prove the Constitution he had done so much to create and ratify was a workable document.

His task was formidable—nothing less than the creation of a government. Everything done or said, even down to such trivia as the title by which Congress should address him (they finally decided on "the President"), set a precedent. As an added difficulty, Washington had to cope at first with the executive departments of the old Articles of Confederation government. The heads of these departments—Foreign Affairs, War, Post Office, and Treasury—reported to Congress, not to the chief executive. A brusque assertion of authority could have been fatal to the relationship between the President and Congress. Here, as in a hundred other matters, Washington displayed his realistic wisdom.

He began by announcing he did not feel at the outset that it was "expedient" to make an official demand for reports from these departments. He let them go on reporting to Congress. He went assiduously to work, reading their files and dispatches, and within three months asked the men

Washington took the oath of office as the first president of the United States on April 30, 1789, in New York City.

in charge for a summary that would give him a
"full precise and general idea" of their work.
Then, without so much as a ruffle of protest, he
quietly took charge of the foreign affairs department because this was a power specifically
granted to him in the Constitution. In the next
few months, he slowly extended his control over
the other departments. While Congress debated
whether to give the President power to remove
the heads of these departments once they were
appointed under the new government, Washington was demonstrating the wisdom of executive control by practicing it under their noses.

Though he was firmly convinced of the need
for a strong executive, Washington was at first
ready to "consult" with Congress on such things
as appropriations and foreign policy. He even
went into the Senate chamber and sat by while
the Vice President read a presidential recommendation on how to pacify the restless Creek Indians. He was dismayed to find himself swiftly
involved in a Senate debate, which ended in a
resolution to postpone the whole matter. "This,"
he said ruefully, "defeats every purpose of my
coming here." That rebuff and an appearance he
made before a Senate committee to defend an
appointment where he very nearly lost his temper, convinced Washington that the President

should keep his distance from Congress and communicate in writing or by sending deputies to represent and defend his policies. He proceeded to create this basic pattern for our government, without bruising sensitive congressional egos.

At least as ticklish was the job of making hundreds of federal appointments, from revenue collectors at the nation's ports to federal district attorneys to justices of the Supreme Court. There was no dearth of applicants. Military heroes and former presidents of the Continental Congress wrote unabashedly declaring their eagerness for a slice of the federal pie. James Wilson of Pennsylvania, one of the signers of the Declaration of Independence, blandly expressed a readiness to become Chief Justice. Washington's nephew, Bushrod, a mere twenty-seven, felt he deserved a job as United States District Attorney for Virginia. To such importunings, Washington repeated a declaration he had made when he was leaving Mount Vernon to take over the government. Influences of "amity or blood" would be considered a minus, not a plus, in a man's chances for office.

Nothing, in Washington's view, was more important than the establishment of a sound federal court system. He spent hours pondering his list of possible Supreme Court judges, boiling it down from several hundred to thirty-five final contenders. He then decided that it was essential to have a geographic distribution, to give decisions the best possible chance of acceptance. He therefore chose the six justices (all that were permitted under the original act of Congress) from the six most populous states: Massachusetts, New York, Pennsylvania, Maryland, Virginia, and South Carolina. For the post of Chief Justice, which Washington called ''the key stone of our political fabric,'' he chose John Jay of New York, a man of unimpeachable integrity and legal reputation.

Not one of Washington's judicial appointments was rejected by the Senate. He did almost as well with his other appointments, following the same policy of geographical spread so that no state could complain of favoritism. He also managed to show no mean skill at politics. For Attorney General, he chose fellow Virginian Edmund Randolph, who had opposed the Constitution. By converting an ex-foe into a member of his cabinet, Washington neatly muffled much lingering resentment against the federal charter in his native state.

For the rest of his cabinet, Washington showed a distinct preference for brains. He chose Thomas Jefferson as Secretary of State and Alexander

Hamilton as Secretary of the Treasury. Young men both, they were undeniably brilliant—too brilliant, Washington eventually discovered, to tolerate each other's presence at the summit of power. In the beginning they gave Washington invaluable and wholehearted assistance in creating a coherent foreign policy and internal economic stability. To their counsels the President added the steady if not as formidable intelligence of his trusted and trustworthy old artillery chief, Henry Knox, as Secretary of War. Washington early instituted the habit of consulting and debating with these men before reaching any important decision. He was also not in the least shy about picking the brains of others, outside the cabinet, notably Congressman James Madison. "I am very troublesome," he wrote Madison, apologizing for seeking his advice so often. "But you must excuse me. Ascribe it to friendship and confidence."

By the time Congress adjourned on September 29th, 1789, Washington could write his friend Gouverneur Morris,". . . National government is organized and as far as my information goes, to the satisfaction of all parties." Events within and without the United States soon made it clear how badly the nation needed the strength and decision Washington brought to the Presidency.

When 7,000 farmers of western Pennsylvania

decided to shoot and assault federal agents rather than pay taxes on their highly profitable whiskey stills, Washington assembled an army, put Lighthorse Harry Lee at its head, and quickly annihilated this abortive rebellion. When the frontier Indians defeated a poorly trained and poorly led American army, Washington chose the best of his remaining Revolutionary generals, Anthony Wayne, ordered the War Department and Treasury Department to give Wayne everything he wanted, and watched him secure the Northwest Territory for American settlement and haul down the British flag in Detroit.

Washington was keenly aware that in the power and prestige of the Presidency lay America's best hope of unity. During his two terms he made sure no one infringed on it. One anecdote that recalled his jousts with British generals over his proper title occurred when Washington made a state visit to Massachusetts, John Hancock was the governor, and the official plan for the visit called for Hancock to greet Washington in his rooms, followed by a state dinner at Hancock's residence. Only a few minutes before the first meeting, Hancock sent word he was ''indisposed.'' Washington instantly saw that his old enemy in the Continental Congress wanted to emphasize the sovereignty of Massachusetts by

29

making the President visit him first. Without a word of reproach, Washington coolly canceled the state dinner and ate in his rooms. The next day Hancock sent a flood of emissaries babbling apologies. When he received word that "the President of the United States" would be available from one P.M. until two P.M., Governor Hancock appeared within the hour to pay his respects to the Presidency.

These state visits gave the country a chance to see the President in action—and with Washington the action was often more than they could handle. Visiting Providence, Rhode Island, he took a four-hour stroll. One congressman who tried to keep up with him moaned that it "completely fatigued the company which formed his escort." The visits also gave Washington an opportunity to affirm the sense of brotherhood that had united Americans of all creeds and sections during the Revolutionary War. Visiting the Jewish synagogue at Newport, he declared, "The government of the United States . . . gives to bigotry no sanction, to persecution no assistance, requires only that they who live under its protection should demean themselves as good citizens."

By far the greatest crisis of Washington's Presidency was the struggle to preserve neutrality between Britain and Revolutionary France in the war which erupted in 1793. The passions which this conflict aroused in the American people almost tore the nation apart. It divided Washington's cabinet: Jefferson siding with France, Hamilton with England. There were moments when it seemed to threaten Washington's life.

The French rebels had guillotined Louis XVI, with whom America had made the treaty of alliance, attacked England, and called for ''a war of all peoples against all kings.'' France's new rulers arrogantly demanded that the infant American republic enter the war as a partisan of liberty. No man had risked more for liberty than George Washington; but he was not the sort of man who plunged into a war simply because someone shouted a slogan. He replied that the treaty of alliance provided for mutual support only if France or America were attacked. In this war France was the aggressor. Moreover, the government with which America had signed the treaty was now totally defunct. Finally, the bulk of American trade was still with England. To go to war would be a death blow to the infant American economy. America, Washington informed the chagrined Thomas Jefferson, would maintain a ''strict neutrality.''

The French and their supporters did everything in their power to make him change his mind. They attacked Washington in the public press. They sent mobs swarming into Philadelphia's streets. Finally "Citizen" Edmond Genêt, ambassador from the new French government, landed in Charleston, Carolina, and proceeded to act as if he, not Washington, was running the country. He commissioned privateers to attack British shipping; planned an invasion of Canada from the Northwest Territory; discussed raising a frontier army to attack Spain in Florida and Louisiana; and authorized French consuls in American ports to act as judges in the disposition of captured British vessels. He also launched a network of "Jacobin Clubs"—not unlike communist cells of today.

En route to Philadelphia Genêt was hailed by tumultuously cheering crowds; prominent citizens rushed to have dinner with him. Washington received him with frigid formality when he finally got around to presenting his credentials to the President (five weeks after his arrival in the country). The thirty-year-old Genêt protested the President's lack of enthusiasm, and his supporters in the press lectured Washington: "Let me caution you, sir, redeem yourself in the eyes of your people."

Genêt continued to act with almost unbelievable arrogance. He demanded that Washington

release two Americans who had sailed on a privateer and had been arrested in Philadelphia for
breach of the national peace. ''I live in a round of
parties,'' he wrote home. ''Old man Washington
cannot forgive my success.''

Meanwhile, the pro-French press swung into
vituperative action. It was led by Philip Freneau,
a Jefferson protégé who had sat out most of the
Revolutionary War in the West Indies. Freneau
compared the President to a crocodile or a hyena.
He pictured Washington as ''lulled by an opiate
of sycophancy'' and warned him that the Presidency was ''temporary,'' implying that there
might be a guillotine waiting for Washington on
the day he ended his term or sooner.

Encouraged by Freneau, other columnists were
even more vicious. The ''Bew letters,'' lewd Tory
forgeries of the Revolutionary War that pictured
Washington as a seducer of his own servants,
were reprinted. This reckless propaganda sent
pro-French mobs storming through the streets,
raising fears for the President's safety. Enraged,
Washington asked Jefferson to call off his curs. He
made it clear that he bitterly resented being written about ''in such exaggerated and indecent
terms as could scarcely be applied to a Nero or
notorious defaulter or even a common pick-
pocket.'' Smarting under one particularly low
fusillade, the presidential temper exploded at a

cabinet meeting with a series of oaths that left politicians and secretaries trembling. ''By God,'' Washington thundered, ''I would rather be in my grave than in this place. I would rather live out my days on my farm than be *emperor of the world!*''

The strain of the situation weakened the sixty-three-year-old President's health. He ran a fever, and Jefferson in a letter to James Madison wept crocodile tears over how poorly he looked. ''He is extremely affected by the attacks made and kept up on him in the public papers. I think he feels these things more than any person I ever yet met with. I am sincerely sorry to see them.''

Genêt, meanwhile, was pirouetting around the country, gathering more ovations, and founding more Jacobin Clubs. Publicly, Washington maintained an icy silence toward the ambassador and his abusive henchmen. The President knew exactly what he was doing; he was, in fact, playing his favorite game. He was waiting for the enemy to make the first wrong move. He had quickly obtained from the American minister in Paris an extensive intelligence report on Genêt, which revealed a fatal weakness for anyone who dared to play for high stakes with George Washington. Genêt had a tendency to talk too much and to the wrong people.

Washington let his cabinet officers deal with Genêt. Steadfastly the President declined to do or say anything that might bring on a popularity contest between himself and the tactless young ambassador. He simply sat back, reinforced his policy with a ringing proclamation of neutrality, and watched Genêt's success go irrevocably to his feverish head.

Genêt now had the effrontery to arm and equip as a privateer a captured British vessel, *Little Sarah*, in the port of Philadelphia, the capital of the United States. This was too much even for the pro-French Jefferson, who warned the reckless ambassador not to let the *Little Sarah* sail. Genêt's contemptuous reply was, ''When ready I shall dispatch her.''

The *Little Sarah* sailed, and the British minister threatened war. Washington now took the nation's foreign policy out of the hands of the vacillating Jefferson. He revoked the diplomatic standing of the French consul in Boston, who had been flouting the Proclamation of Neutrality. In a virulent speech, Genêt threatened to appeal over the President's head to the American people. This was the moment Washington had awaited. Would his fellow citizens support their President or this foreign intruder? Coolly, Washington helped them make up their minds by letting Alexander Hamilton leak to the press the bullying, insulting correspondence Genêt had carried on with the American government since his arrival.

An avalanche of public indignation buried Genêt. City after city held public meetings and forwarded testaments of loyalty to Washington. Now it was a simple matter to ask the French government for their ex-favorite's recall. When his replacement arrived with a warrant for Genêt's arrest, the fallen idol panicked, realizing that he was a prime candidate for the Terror's busy guillotine. With typical magnanimity, Washington permitted his ex-tormentor to remain in America as a private citizen.

For a man who was considered by many to be rather slow (though sound) in his thinking, Washington continuously outwitted French efforts to force the young republic into an open break with England. Another French minister, Pierre Adet, presented a richly ornamented silk flag to Washington. The previous year the American minister in Paris, James Monroe, had unofficially presented an American flag to French legislators, who gave it a permanent place of honor in their hall. In the light of Washington's struggle for neutrality, this was indiscreet of Monroe. Adet eagerly took advantage of the chance to embarrass Washington by returning the compliment. Instead of rebuffing his offer, Washington accepted the tricolor with a speech so flattering and enthusiastic Adet was momentarily bewildered. He heaped superlatives on the French people. ''To call your nation brave were to pronounce but common praise . . . Ages that come will read with astonishment the history of your brillant exploits . . . The French colors," he concluded, "would be deposited in the national archives." It took Adet several days to realize that Washington had hoodwinked him. Instead of being displayed conspicuously in Congress, the flag moldered somewhere in the Department of State.

A sort of climax was reached when a French scholar (and notorious revolutionist) named Constantin Volney asked Washington for a letter of recommendation to ease his progress about the United States. The President forwarded the following diplomatic masterpiece.

> C. Volney
> 　　needs no recommendation from
> 　　　　　　　　　　　　Geo. Washington

A more personal, but equally thorny diplomatic problem during this crisis-filled period was Lafayette. His attempt to ride the tigerish French revolution ended in disaster, and he narrowly escaped being devoured. Forced to flee his own countrymen, the Marquis was captured by the Austrians and flung into prison. Washington did everything in his power to help him, interceding with England and Austria through American diplomats abroad, and depositing 200 guineas of his own money in Amsterdam for the support of his friend's family.

This was difficult enough. Lafayette multiplied Washington's troubles by sending his son, George Washington Lafayette, to America at the height of the neutrality uproar. Washington decided, with the greatest reluctance, that he could not see the young man lest he be accused of favoring the anti-revolutionists in France. He made sure the boy was provided for handsomely in his travels about America. In New York, for instance, he had Alexander Hamilton look after him. Washington was determined, he told Hamilton, "under any circumstances to be in the place of a father and friend to him."

At the end of his second term, Washington took the boy home with him to Mount Vernon, where he and his tutor stayed for over a year until Lafayette was released from prison. A line in Washington's ledger testifies to his generosity. "By Geo. W. Fayette gave for the purpose of his getting himself such small articles of clothing as he might not choose to ask for—a hundred dollars." When they said good-bye, Washington handed him another check for 300 dollars "to defray his exps. to France."

11

A Reputation Lost?

THROUGHOUT HIS PRESIDENCY Washington took a salary of 25,000 dollars a year for expenses. To make ends meet, he was forced to sell more than 60,000 dollars worth of land during his two terms. Worries over money explained in part why Washington spent long hours writing vastly detailed letters back to Mount Vernon in a vain attempt to supervise, at a distance, his often incompetent overseers. One reason Mount Vernon lost money was because Washington refused to sell any of his slaves, although he owned many more than the farm could profitably employ. Washington's attitude toward slavery underwent a slow, steady change in the last half of his life. At the start of the revolution he apparently regarded the "peculiar institution" with the eyes of a typical Virginia proprietor. He owned almost three hundred slaves and treated them well, deploring those who considered blacks "much in the same light as they do rude beasts on the farm."

Conversations with young idealists like Lafayette turned Washington into a steadfast foe of slavery. When one man offered him slaves in settlement of a debt, Washington replied, "I never mean to possess another slave by purchase, it being among my first wishes to see . . . slavery abolished by slow, sure and imperceptible degrees." In 1794 he wrote to another friend, "Were it not then that I am principled against selling Negroes as you would do cattle in the market, I would not in twelve months be possessed of one as a slave."

Billy Lee, Washington's daring master of the hounds, had ridden with him across every Revolutionary battlefield. In later years he broke both his knees in falls and became almost a hopeless cripple. When Washington left to assume the Presidency, Billy begged to go with him, and Washington could not say no. Alas Billy collapsed in Philadelphia and had to be left behind. But Tobias Lear, Washington's secretary, wrote a letter from New York, expressing his chief's deep concern. "The President will thank you to propose to Will to return to Mount Vernon when he can be removed . . . But if he is still anxious to come on here, the President would gratify him . . . He has been an old and faithful servant and this is enough for the President to gratify him in every reasonable wish.''

Washington gave Billy, along with all the other Mount Vernon slaves, his freedom in his last will and testament. But for Billy, crippled and old, Washington made a special proviso. He could stay at Mount Vernon for the rest of his life if he chose to do so. In any case, he received a cash annuity, ''independent of the victuals and clothes he has been accustomed to receive.''

This deep bond between Washington and his slaves continued till the very end of his life. As he gasped for breath, his throat constricted by the infection which was to kill him, one of his personal servants, Christopher, stood for hours beside his bed, tears streaming down his face. Washington could no longer speak, but he motioned to a nearby chair and made it clear he wanted Christopher to rest himself.

At the same time Washington could be more than a little sharp with servants who challenged his authority. One who did so consistently—and got away with it—was the presidential steward, ''Black Sam'' Fraunces. Washington ran his household with the same sharp executive eye that he applied to running the government. (Asked to approve a new chain for a Navy ship, Washington signed the requisition, and added, ''Cannot something be realized from the old chain?'') Black Sam, reputed to have been one of Washington's New York spies during the war, was too much for him. Again and again the President told Sam he spent too much money on food. Sam stoutly replied that he was determined to set a table worthy of the President of the United States. One spring day Sam saw a fine shad, the first of the season. Ignoring the price, he purchased it and it appeared on the breakfast table the following morning. Washington, instantly suspicious, demanded to know the price. When Sam confessed he had paid three dollars for it, Washington became so furious he could not eat it and ordered it removed from the table. Sam served it with a flourish to the servants downstairs and went right on spending the President's money.

Few people remember that during these seven burdensome years Washington and his wife were raising two grandchildren, Nellie and George Washington Parke Custis. Washington had adopted them not long after the death of Jack Custis. Nellie was ten, George eight, when they went to New York in Washington's first term. Martha described Nellie as ''a little wild creature,'' probably made so by the excitement of her first visit to a great city. She swiftly became Wash-

ington's favorite. He constantly bought her presents, including a 1000 dollar piano, and regularly
took her with him on walks and rides. Her girlish
chatter and unflagging spirits undoubtedly were
a sweet relief after the harassments of politics.
Once, he tried to persuade Martha that she was
making Nellie practice the piano too long—often
as much as five hours a day. As in everything else
concerning her children, Martha smiled and went
right on doing it her way.

During Washington's two presidential terms
Nellie grew into a beautiful young woman.
Suitors were soon flocking from all directions, but
Nellie kept them all at arm's length. Apparently
she admired Washington so extravagantly that she
expressed total apathy for the ''youth'' of her day,
and vowed ''never to give herself a moment's
uneasiness on account of any of them.''

Washington could not resist sending her some
fond advice:

> Men and women feel the same inclinations toward
> each other now that they always have done and
> which they will continue to do until there is a new
> order of things and you, as others have done, may
> find perhaps that the passions of your sex are
> easier raised than allayed. Do not therefore boast
> too soon or too strongly of your insensibility to or
> resistance of its powers. In the composition of the
> human frame there is a good deal of inflammable

matter, however dormant it may lie for a time, and like an intimate acquaintance of yours, when the torch is put to it, that which is within you may burst into a blaze.

Washington was, of course, referring to himself. He had fought such inner conflagrations and won. Only a soft melancholy remained when he thought of those long-gone days at Belvoir. Not long after Washington's second term was over, Bryan Fairfax came to tell Washington he was returning to England for a while. Would Washington like to send Sally a letter? Washington welcomed the opportunity and together he and Martha composed a long chatty epistle, full of gossip from the neighborhood. Then Washington added words that were distinctly his own:

> Five and twenty years nearly have passed away since I have considered myself as a permanent resident at this place . . . During this period so many important events have occurred and such changes in men and things have taken place, as the compass of a letter would give you but an inadequate idea of. None of which events, however, nor all of them together, have been able to eradicate from my mind the recollections of those happy moments, the happiest in my life, which I have enjoyed in your company.

Washington urged Sally to come home and spend "the evening of your life" with old friends and relations. Sally chose to remain in England. More than fifty years after her death, relatives brought her letters back to the United States, and the story of Washington's secret love was revealed to an astonished nation.

However, Washington's nostalgia never cast a shadow on his devotion to Martha, which deepened during his presidential years. The courageous woman of the war years revealed still another side of her personality, one that played a vital role in smoothing her husband's political path. Straining to give the Presidency the dignity it so badly needed, Washington tended to make his receptions and public dinners extremely formal. It could well have cost him his popularity, but Martha had receptions of her own for wives of congressmen and other officials and these she ran in her own warm, good-natured way. She made scores of friends for Washington, humanizing him in the eyes of his guests at a time when he was afraid to unbend. "Mrs. Washington is one of those unassuming characters which create love and esteem," wrote Abigail Adams, a woman with a sharp eye for human foibles. "A most becoming pleasantness sits upon her countenance."

Martha also played an important part in nursing Washington through two serious illnesses.

Early in the Presidency, he was operated on for a tumor in his thigh. He ran a high fever for weeks and was in acute pain day and night. Two years later he contracted pneumonia and at one point was given up by his doctors. Again Martha's soothing presence helped him through a long convalescence.

Throughout his Presidency, old soldiers often knocked on Washington's door, certain of a warm reception from their former commander-in-chief. Though Washington did not have time to see them all, there was a standing order that any veteran was to be served a good meal in the kitchen and sent away with a few dollars in his pocket. One ex-soldier with a thick brogue and plenty of nerve showed up during one of Washington's formal receptions. The doorkeeper, an ex-Hessian named German John, tried to bar him. The veteran became incensed at finding a former enemy guarding the General's house and announced he would wait in the vestibule until he saw the General personally.

Not wanting to create a scene, German John let him stay. The politicians and diplomats swept by him to shake the President's hand and drink his punch. Ignoring their stares, the veteran sat it out. Hours later, when the last guest finally departed, he was still there. The President was on his way to bed when German John asked what he should do about the intruder. Washington came downstairs and shook the man's hand, asked where he had fought and chatted with him about war days. As they said good-bye, the President slipped him the money he was hoping to get. On his way out the Irishman shook the coins under German John's nose and crowed triumphantly. "Didn't I tell you His Excellency wouldn't forget an old soldier?"

In the last months of the Presidency, Washington had to endure another storm of public agitation over the commercial treaty that John Jay signed with England. In the opinion of Jefferson and his French-loving supporters, Jay made more concessions than he gained. There was a certain amount of truth in this claim, but Washington, ever the realist, believed it was the best possible treaty that could be obtained and it was badly needed by the nation's struggling economy. He backed it firmly.

The abuse he endured was almost unbelievable. Pro-French newspaper editors sneered at "his farce of disinterestedness," and "his stately journeyings through the American continent in search of personal incense." Another scribbler declared, "Had you obtained promotion . . . after Braddock's defeat, your sword would have been drawn against your country" and vowed that "posterity will in vain search for the monuments of wisdom in your administration." A third accused Washington of authorizing "the robbery and ruin of the remnants of his own army" and damned "the vileness of the adulation which has been paid to him."

Perhaps the bitterest attack came from Tom Paine, the famed author of *Common Sense*. Washington had helped Paine get a job in 1782 and had tried to get the Virginia legislature to vote him a pension or a grant of land. When Paine published his "Rights of Man" he dedicated it to Washington. But when Paine's friends tried to make him the Postmaster General, a job for which he was totally unsuited, Washington turned him down. Paine went to Europe, became involved with the French Revolution, and ended up in jail. Since Paine had resigned his American citizenship and had become a French citizen, Washington decided he could not interfere on his behalf. Brooding over these two decisions, Paine now charged Washington with being "the patron of fraud." He ended his attack with an hysterical denunciation, "Treacherous in private friendship and a hypocrite in public life, the world will be puzzled to decide whether you are an apostate or an impostor; whether you have abandoned good principles or whether you ever had any."

The prosperity which resulted from the British

treaty soon made these attackers look silly. However, for a man who valued his reputation and good name as intensely as Washington, these scurrilous assaults were hard to bear. With all these harassments, Washington found time in the closing days of his term for one of those small acts of thoughtfulness that received no publicity. John Quincy Adams, the son of the incoming President, had already proven himself abroad as one of America's best diplomats. Washington knew that Adams was going to find it politically difficult to appoint his son to an important post. He wrote a letter to the President-elect, expressing ''a strong hope that you will not withhold merited promotion . . . because he is your son. For . . . I give it as my decided opinion that Mr. Adams is the most valuable public character we have abroad and that he will prove himself to be the ablest of all our diplomatic corps.'' Such a testimonial, of course, was a priceless political weapon should Adams need to defend himself with it.

It was during this last year of the Presidency that Gilbert Stuart painted the portrait of Washington which serves as the image on the dollar bill and was made the national official portrait at the two hundredth anniversary of Washington's birth in 1932. It was a poor choice. While Washington sat for this portrait, he was suffering because of an extremely poor set of false teeth, so ill-fitting they could be held in place only by placing bands of cotton inside his mouth. The result, inevitably, is a distortion of Washington's normal expression. Washington's family never considered the portrait realistic. The eyes, one of them declared, were too soulful. They lacked Washington's "quick and knowing" look. Careful measurements derived from a life mask done by another artist make it clear that Stuart's proportions, particularly the distance between the nose and chin, are wrong.

Stuart, who was something of an amateur psychologist, studied Washington closely while he painted. He declared that he saw on the President's face "features . . . indicative of the strongest and most ungovernable passions. Had he been born in the forests, he would have been the fiercest man among the savage tribes." Jane Stuart, the painter's daughter, repeated this estimate to a number of people. It finally got back to Washington via his old cavalry commander, Light Horse Harry Lee.

"I saw your portrait the other day, a capital likeness," said Lee. "But Stuart says you have a tremendous temper."

"Upon my word," said Martha, who was having breakfast with her husband. "Mr. Stuart takes a great deal on himself to make such a remark."

"But stay, my dear lady," said General Lee. "He added that the President had it under wonderful control."

With a twinkle in his eyes, Washington nodded. "He's right."

On Washington's last day in office, a pro-French scribbler sneered: "The man who is the source of all the misfortunes of our country is this day reduced to a level with his fellow citizens, and is no longer possessed of power to multiply evils upon the United States. If ever there was a period for rejoicing, this is the moment."

If history were written by newspapers, one might conclude from this vitriol that Washington's worst fears had come true. He had gambled the good name he had won on the Revolution's fields and lost it in the back-alley gougings of partisan politics. But history is written in many places. One of the most important is in the hearts of the people. On this last day, the people said farewell to George Washington in a way that was uniquely right, both for them and for him.

After the inauguration Washington went home and put his papers in order. Then, before returning to Mount Vernon where he would live as a farmer until his death in 1799, he decided to walk to the Francis Hotel, where the new President, John Adams, was staying, to pay his respects. He

In this "official" portrait, painted by Gilbert Stuart in 1797, President Washington's expression is said to be distorted because of ill-fitting false teeth.

was plain George Washington now, neither general nor president, and there was no need for anyone to fawn upon him. Suddenly behind him the streets were full of people. "An immense company," one eyewitness called them, "going as one man in total silence as escort all the way."

At the door of the hotel, Washington turned and looked at them, his cheeks wet with tears. "No man ever saw him so moved," declared a witness. For a long moment he stood face-to-face with his people in that solemn silence. Then he turned, and, when the door closed behind him, a great smothered sigh went through the crowd, something between a sob and a groan.

It was the tribute of grief from the voiceless common man who knew that he was saying good-bye to his greatest friend.

For Further Reading

Davidson, Margaret. *The Adventures of George Washington*. New York: Scholastic, 1989.

Hilton, Suzanne. *The World of Young George Washington*. New York: Walker, 1987.

Kent, Zachary. *George Washington*. Chicago: Children's Press, 1986.

Meltzer, Milton. *George Washington and the Birth of Our Nation*. New York: Watts, 1986.

Index